7927

HAND,
HEART,
& MIND

HAND,
HEART,
& MIND

The Story
of the Education of
America's Deaf People

LOU ANN WALKER

DIAL BOOKS NEW YORK

In the 1980's a movement began in which people writing about the subject of deafness used a capital "D" for "Deaf" when referring to those who consider themselves to be culturally Deaf. A person who is culturally Deaf is someone who strongly identifies with Deaf people and who uses sign language as the major form of communication when talking with Deaf people. The words "deaf" and "Deaf" in this book are an attempt to honor those distinctions made by culturally Deaf people. In some cases the rule is difficult to apply.

In addition, many people object to the term "the deaf." They insist that people should be considered as human beings first, and deaf or Deaf second. I have tried to use the word "deaf" as an adjective throughout this book, discussing "the deaf world," "deaf students," "deaf leaders," "deaf people," and so forth.

Published by Dial Books
A Division of Penguin Books USA Inc.
375 Hudson Street
New York, New York 10014

Library of Congress Cataloging in Publication Data
Walker, Lou Ann.
Hand, heart, and mind : the story of the education of America's
deaf people / Lou Ann Walker.—1st ed.
p. cm.
Includes bibliographical references and index.
Summary: Focuses on efforts to educate deaf people in the United
States, from colonial times to the present.
ISBN 0-8037-1225-1
1. Deaf—Education—United States—History—[1. Deaf—Education—History.] I. Title.
HV2530.W35 1994 371.91′2′0973—dc20 92-45631 CIP AC

Special thanks to Frank G. Bowe, Ph.D., Professor, Department of Counseling, Research,
Special Education, and Rehabilitation at Hofstra University, for checking the facts in this book.

FRONTISPIECE: *This statue by Daniel Chester French shows Thomas Hopkins Gallaudet teaching the manual alphabet to Alice Cogswell, the first student at the American School for the Deaf.*
Permission of the American School for the Deaf

To my parents,
Gale and Doris Walker,
who care passionately about education

Contents

HAND,
HEART,
& MIND

Foreword

In 1988 a momentous event occurred in the Deaf world. Deaf students spoke up for their rights—and the entire world listened. Since its beginnings Gallaudet University, the world's only liberal arts university specifically for deaf people, had had a hearing person as its president. When the board of trustees ignored the deaf people who had applied and chose yet another hearing person for the job in March 1988, deaf students and teachers at the university were outraged. Why should hearing people govern them? Why did the hearing world have to act as if deaf people were second-class citizens?

For one week students, later joined by teachers, closed down the university. They named their movement "Deaf President Now!"—DPN for short. Deaf people came to Washington, D.C., from all over the world to lend their support. Excitement filled the air as hands signed vividly. Students held up banners that read, "Deaf Pride!"

For a week the national news was full of reports about the Gallaudet revolt. Hearing people all around the country were forced to take heed. And in the end members of the board of trustees admitted they had made a terrible mistake. If deaf people could get advanced college degrees and work in high-level government and private jobs, the trustees decided, then they should be able to run their own university too. I. King Jordan, a man who had become deaf when he was twenty-one years old, was named president of the university.

Dr. Jordan had been a professor of psychology at Gallaudet for many years, and he was a popular man on campus. "We will no longer accept limits on what we can achieve," he said in his acceptance speech.

The story of the education of deaf people in America has two parts. First, deaf people needed the tools to communicate, both with each other and with the rest of society. After they won the right to these basic skills, they could work to establish their civil rights.

Few deaf people think of themselves as handicapped. What they have is a language disability. Not being able to hear from infancy makes it very hard to learn spoken and written language. As babies our brains are like tape recorders, taking in all the language around us. The patterns of sounds people hear are what they use for building language, from the first time a baby says "Mama" to when he or she speaks in sentences. Deaf or hearing, if we don't have language stored in the memory banks of our brain computers, then it is much, much harder later on to make sentences.

It took centuries for hearing people to make any real effort to provide deaf people with the opportunity to study written and spoken language. Gradually, as deaf people acquired those skills—whether through speaking, reading lips (also called lipreading), writing, or signing—they could work toward the goal of having the same rights as other people. Together, the two parts of their story tell of a civil rights struggle— a fight for the same educational opportunities that other Americans take as their birthright.

Ever since the Gallaudet uprising, the world has changed significantly for young and old Deaf people alike. Congress has passed laws reinforcing the rights of Deaf people. Older Deaf people who had in the past been made to feel ashamed of their deafness could feel proud. Younger Deaf people suddenly realized the world was full of possibilities for them. They had more opportunities. They could fight against discrimination.

Students who led the protest are continuing in their efforts to make the world a better place for deaf people. One young person went to law school; another enrolled in graduate school to study public policy. Several worked for members of Congress. One of their goals is to teach others that deaf people are not different from the hearing.

The strides made by Deaf people in the past few years seem even more remarkable when we realize the difficulties they have faced. The question of *how* to educate deaf people has always seemed to spark angry arguments. This history of the education of deaf people is a challenging story. It is full of setbacks. There have been many terrible defeats, but also thrilling triumphs. There have even been a few mysteries—as well as some of the angriest fights and arguments that have ever taken place in education.

From the Time of the Ancients to the Middle Ages

Few people realize how many ways our everyday lives have been changed as a direct result of deaf people. The football huddle was invented during a nineteenth-century college football game at Gallaudet. Players needed to discuss their next moves, but wanted to hide what they were signing from the opposing team. The telephone came about because of Alexander Graham Bell's interest in deaf people. His mother was deaf, and his experiments began as a way to devise a technological device for deaf people. He wanted to make words fly through the air.

We take these contributions to our culture for granted today—but it is only in the past few centuries that, outside their own circles of family and friends, deaf people gained recognition from society at large.

Our story begins in ancient Greece over two thousand years ago. In the time of antiquity, people who were deaf used pantomime signs to get their meaning across. Great thinkers such as the philosopher Socrates were fascinated by the idea of talking without using words. In fact, Socrates once said:

> I think, therefore, that if we wished to
> signify that which is upwards and light, we
> should raise our hands toward the heavens; . . .
> but that if we wished to indicate things downwards
> and heavy, we should point with our hands to
> the earth. And again, if we were desirous of
> signifying a running horse, or any other animal,
> . . . we would fashion the gestures and
> figures of our bodies, as near as possible to
> a similitude of those things.

Socrates's comments, made around 386 B.C., are probably the first ones ever written about sign language. Nevertheless, the philosophers of the time didn't think deaf people could be taught to communicate. Around 355 B.C., the philosopher and scientist Aristotle said that people born deaf "become senseless and incapable of reason." In other words he felt that anyone born deaf could not think. Obviously today we know that is not true. But the ancient Greeks and Romans were still discovering how our bodies work, and they thought that hearing and speech were connected in the brain. They assumed if you could not hear, you could never talk.

Surprisingly, around A.D. 77, a Roman scholar, Pliny the Elder, wrote about a young deaf boy named Quintus Pedius. The boy's father was a consul, or chief magistrate, of the Roman Republic, and was one of Julius Caesar's heirs. Caesar Augustus, the other heir, was interested in young Quintus Pedius and ordered that he take painting lessons. Apparently the boy became quite a good artist.

But it would be hundreds of years before the first recorded instance of someone educating a deaf person. In A.D. 721 the Venerable Bede, an English cleric, wrote about St. John of Beverly "loosening" the tongue of a young man who had formerly not been able to speak.

Because deaf people were not being taught to read and write, no one thought they were important enough to write down their history—and of course no deaf person had the skills to do this. Great philosophers and scholars thought about the condition of deaf people, but often their conclusions caused as much harm as good. St. Paul said, "Faith comes through hearing," and St. Augustine said of deafness, "This impairment prevents faith." As a result, for centuries many Catholic priests said that deaf people could not be Christians because they could not "hear the word of God," which meant their souls could not be saved. Some early Christian weddings were performed in sign language, but later the Catholic Church refused to allow deaf people to take communion because they were incapable of confessing out loud.

Doctors used many odd treatments to try to cure

deafness. They would blow trumpets into people's ears or ring loud bells. They would pour different kinds of oils, milk, even garlic juice and eel fat right into their patients' ears.

The prejudices against deaf people lasted for thousands of years. There must have been many, many examples of deaf people being clever in one field or another—yet since they had no education, the rest of the world simply overlooked their native abilities. In fact, it was not until the 1500's that an Italian doctor finally said that deaf people were capable of using their minds.

Through the Middle Ages, deaf people were not allowed to marry or to own property. In 1575 a Spanish lawyer, Lasso, announced that being deaf did not render people automatically unintelligent and that they should have the right to bear children.

Around that same time there was a Spanish boy who had become deaf during an illness when he was about three years old. A priest tutored him in art, and the boy, whose real name was Juan F. X. Navaretta, was so talented that when he was just a teenager, he was sent to study with the famous painter Titian in Italy.

Juan, who was known as El Mudo—Spanish for "The Mute"—returned to Spain when he was in his thirties. At that time King Philip II had hired and fired a number of painters to decorate the walls of the Escorial Palace. Finally the king's chaplain suggested the king invite El Mudo to enter a competition for the work. El Mudo's painting of the baptism of Christ was so accomplished that he was asked to become a court painter, a high honor.

El Mudo had a well-developed sense of humor. Once, while painting a scene of a saint who was martyred, the artist used the likeness of the king's secretary, whom he disliked very much, as the model for an executioner. The secretary begged the king to order the face changed, but the king, who was very fond of El Mudo, refused. King Philip II even stopped El Mudo from destroying his own paintings when the artist felt they were not worthy of his work.

It was probably fairly easy for deaf people to work on farms and in homes through the Middle Ages. Someone could demonstrate the work that had to be done. But as reading and writing became more important, starting in the late sixteenth century, deaf people came up against barriers.

The first real efforts to educate deaf people began around 1550 when Pablo Ponce de Leon, a monk from Spain, taught deaf children in a monastery in San Salvador. A deaf man had wanted to become a monk but was turned down because of his deafness. Ponce de Leon worked with him until he was able to read and speak well enough to enter the Benedictine order. Later, Ponce de Leon founded a school north of Madrid for deaf sons born of noble parents. We know very little about Ponce de Leon's methods, but we do know that the people who wrote about his work disagreed about whether he used signs or whether he used the oral method, teaching children to lip-read and speak. Some say he used signs. Others say he did not. We may never know.

Ponce de Leon was trying to save the souls of deaf people he taught, but the wealthy families who sent their deaf sons to him had another strong reason for wanting to educate the children. There was so much intermarriage in royal and noble families that a fairly large percentage of babies were born handicapped or deaf. Only by learning to speak could a deaf son inherit his father's estate and keep the family name and fortune intact. Because one tutor usually worked intensively with one child, the pupils often did well.

After Ponce de Leon's death two of his followers took over his work, Juan Pablo Bonet and Manuel Ramirez de Carrion. In 1620 Bonet, who had been in the secret service to the king, published the first book on the education of deaf people, and in his book he revealed his method. He started by using a one-handed manual alphabet—a revolutionary step. The entire family had to learn to use the alphabet. Then Bonet built spoken language, first in sounds, then in syllables, and finally in entire words, by using the letters of the alphabet. Bonet may have stolen many of his ideas from Ramirez; thus arose the first controversy in the teaching of deaf people. It is also possible that the families whom these men taught had many deaf members who were used to communicating with each other and who were actually helping their teachers learn how to teach. But at last a manual alphabet had been described and shown to others. That Spanish fingerspelling is the basis of European and American fingerspelling today.

Still, Ramirez de Carrion was a rather cruel taskmaster. He taught a boy who was a prince of Italy by sometimes starving him, and other times beating the soles of his feet. Nevertheless, the boy, who was very intelligent, grew up able to speak several languages, and he was frequently consulted on important governmental matters.

Slowly the language of signs captured the interest of scholars in Europe. In the 1600's people in Spain, Italy, Scotland, and England wrote about sign language. And in 1700 Johann Ammon, a Swiss doctor, developed a way to teach speech and lipreading to deaf people. As writers and educators became more curious about the deaf, they began to reach out to them. But very few were receiving instruction. Most of those who did were the children of extremely wealthy families. There were still many breakthroughs to come.

The French Deaf Community

In the mid-eighteenth century, schools for deaf children were established in Edinburgh, Scotland; Leipzig, Germany; and Paris, France.

In 1760 a man named Thomas Braidwood began teaching his first deaf pupil in Edinburgh. (Members of his family would also be responsible for opening schools in England.) The Braidwood School was expensive and rather exclusive, which meant that many children were turned away. Girls learned needlework or how to be maids or laundresses. Boys received a wider education and were taught to be shoemakers or tailors.

Although the Braidwood family kept many of their training techniques secret, we know that the schools stressed the oral method, teaching students lipreading and speech. Some children who were hearing, but had difficulties with speech, also attended the school. Teachers did, however, use the manual alphabet. The son of the school's founder, John Braidwood, went to the United States to teach deaf children. Braidwood, an alcoholic, tried repeatedly between 1805 and 1818 to found a school for deaf children in America, but he failed each time.

Samuel Heinicke, a former German soldier, had taught a few people beginning around 1755. Heinicke said he believed strongly in using the oral method, although we have discovered that he did use the manual alphabet as well as some gestures with his pupils. He also wrote textbooks for his students. Around 1778 he founded a public school in Leipzig with the support of Frederick Augustus, the prince of Saxony. Oralism—using lipreading and speaking without any signs—came to be called "the German method."

Heinicke was not a very likable man, and only he and his son, who worked with him, really knew what his teaching techniques were. When one man wrote to Heinicke asking for advice, Heinicke wrote back that he would help—if the man would pay an enormous sum of money. After Heinicke died, his secret method for teaching deaf people to speak was revealed: In addition to the senses of touch and vision, he added taste. For *a* he poured vinegar on a student's tongue. For *ie* he used pure water. Sugar water was used for *o*, olive oil for *ou*, and absinthe, a strongly flavored type of liquor, for *e*. We don't know how successful this rather odd approach was, but we do know that while students learned some speech, many seemed to lose their abilities later.

Meanwhile, in Paris, a very different kind of school

was being formed by Charles-Michel de l'Épée—a religious man, or abbé. Abbé de l'Épée had no parish. Instead, he lived on an allowance from his family, which was quite wealthy. (His father had been an architect for King Louis XIV at Versailles.) But he was a man of strong principles, and he believed passionately in doing right for poor people.

One day in the 1760's he went into a home in a grindingly poor area of Paris. We don't know why he went there, but we know that when he entered the home and said good day to the two daughters who were doing needlework in the living room, they did not look up. Épée thought they were very shy and sat down to wait for the mother's return. When she came back from her errands, she explained to him that her twin fifteen-year-old daughters were deaf. Her husband had died several years before, and the daughters did needlepoint to earn money for food. The neighborhood priest had been using engravings of the saints to try to teach the girls about religion, but he had died before they had been able to take communion.

Suddenly Épée had a calling. He wanted to teach the girls.

He began by showing them objects, then printed words. He had no idea how to teach abstract ideas like *God* until he realized that he should learn the sign language the girls were already using. Épée acknowledged that the signs were a language, but like educators for the next two centuries, he thought the language had no grammar.

Soon Épée was teaching other deaf people. Many of his students were very smart, and some went on to have good careers. They were often expert at copying down French, but they were weak when it came to *using* the written French language. And the grammatical signs that Abbé de l'Épée added often made sign language awkward. The verb for *give,* for example, might require five separate signs. The beauty of a natural sign language is its sleekness and simplicity.

In Paris in the 1760's Charles-Michel de l'Épée established the first free school in the world for deaf children from all backgrounds. It would eventually be called the National Institute for Deaf-Mutes and was located in a house owned by his family. Some have called Épée the "liberator" of deaf people: Through the dictionary that he wrote and the school that he founded, sign language began to be standardized in France. Students and teachers trained by Épée would go to the provinces employing the sign language they had used in Paris. He was a gentle soul who, it is said, never took money for teaching the deaf.

Some mistakenly credited Épée with inventing sign language. He did not. He took the sign language his students were using naturally—and he did believe that the way they used gestures was indeed a language—and he employed that language to teach them academic subjects, including stylishly written French. To that natural language, Épée added the signs used by Cistercian monks who had taken vows of silence. He also invented certain grammatical signs for the language, and he called his method "signes methodiques" or methodical signs.

Eventually teaching with the use of sign language was called "the French method." It was finally possible for deaf people to communicate more fully.

There was a very large mystery connected with Épée's National Institute that to this day has not been solved.

One day in 1773 a deaf boy was found wandering the roads and brought into a mental institution. The blond, blue-eyed boy, unable to communicate, was tormented by the people in the institution. After two years when the boy became very sick, he was taken to a Parisian hospital where a nun cared for him. As he was recuperating, the nun introduced him to Abbé de l'Épée.

The boy, whose name was Joseph, told the abbé in sign language that he had wealthy parents and servants; that his father had a limp; and that one day a man had put him on a horse, put a mask over his head, and then abandoned him far from his home. The abbé took the boy into his school, then tried to verify the story by sending posters around France. He received many letters, but none of them seemed to be about Joseph. The abbé did get a letter from one woman who said she had witnessed the son of the count of Solar being led away by one of the countess's servants. She never saw the boy—whose name was Joseph—again. She had been told that on his way to take the waters as a cure for his deafness, the boy had fallen ill and died. After so many false leads, the abbé did not pay attention to that letter. A few years passed.

Abbé de l'Épée loved to give public demonstrations to show the talents of his pupils. Many considered Épée to have worked miracles. During one of these demonstrations, a woman in the audience jumped up and pointed to Joseph, saying, "It's the count of Solar!" The woman had worked for relatives of the Solar family. Although the boy's mother and father had died, she said that the family's former maid could confirm the boy's identity.

The maid was sent for. She hugged the boy, saying that he was indeed Joseph, the count of Solar. Joseph was taken to his hometown, and even his grandfather verified that he was really the young count. The count's sister, Caroline, brought to meet the boy, at first didn't recognize him. Only after talking in their particular signs and after the boy reminded her of events from childhood did she say he was her brother. As further proof, the boy had the unusual extra tooth that many in the Solar family had. Joseph also had a birthmark on his bottom. The boy's baby nurse and teacher confirmed that it was identical to the birthmark on the young count.

Now the plot thickens. Joseph had been led away by Cazeaux, a law student, who worked for the countess and returned after seven months saying that the boy had died of smallpox and was buried in his own family's tomb. (The countess had always thought it was embarrassing to have a deaf son. Cazeaux, by the way, was a handsome man who was quite fond of the countess.) After the countess's husband died, she and Cazeaux had a child together, which they gave up for adoption. She died not long after.

The case became the talk of Paris. When officials started to investigate the matter of Joseph, they found the death certificate for the boy Cazeaux had buried was full of blank spaces, and the words "Comte de Solar" looked to have been added at a later time. Cazeaux, of course, insisted that the boy called Joseph in Paris was not the real count.

Cazeaux pointed out that the boy in Abbé de l'Épée's school was found wandering the roads a full month *before* he had left Toulouse to take the count for a cure. In court Épée deduced that the countess and Cazeaux must have hired a stand-in after Cazeaux had already taken the boy away and abandoned him. The court ordered that the tomb where the boy who had had smallpox was buried be opened.

Everyone was astonished when a child's skeleton was found in the tomb. A doctor examined the skeleton and found, also to everyone's surprise, that the head had the famous Solar extra tooth. The court made a very odd decision: Cazeaux was not guilty, but Joseph was indeed the count of Solar.

And what happened eventually? In 1792, after Épée had died, Cazeaux and Caroline, who had lost half her fortune to Joseph, appealed the case. The second court overturned part of the earlier court's ruling. It ruled that Joseph was not the count after all. Joseph went on to become a soldier, and legend has it that he died on the battlefield when he could not hear the bugle blow to signal a retreat. Cazeaux and the sister, Caroline de Solar, married. To make the whole case even more complicated, lawyers for *both* sides changed their minds after the case was over! In his will, the lawyer from the original case who prosecuted Cazeaux left Cazeaux and Caroline his house and money. The lawyer who originally defended Cazeaux later told friends that he believed Joseph had truly been the count!

Épée was no stranger to controversy, and it seems very fitting that the first clash of oral methods versus signing methods for teaching deaf people arose between Épée and Heinicke. In 1782 these two men, after furious debate over teaching methods, asked the Zurich Academy to judge which was better. The academy referees sided with Épée, but because Heinicke was so jealously secretive and refused to tell the referees much about his own method, it couldn't really be called a fair fight.

From the beginning critics of the oral method said that emphasizing speech with deaf children meant that the children had less time for academic studies. Speech training for deaf people requires constant, lifelong practice. Furthermore, opponents of oralism claimed deaf people trained in this method could not communicate as easily with each other.

On the other hand critics of the signing method said that people trained only to sign can never enter into society at large, and that deaf people would remain stigmatized for the rest of their lives because of the enormous communication gap with the rest of the world.

It would be hundreds of years before educators took two major factors into account when trying to decide the best method for teaching deaf students. One was the age at which students lost their hearing. People who become deaf or hard of hearing later in life often express how frustrated they feel at being cut off from the rest of society. But often the successes that the early educators for deaf students had were with those who lost their hearing later in life because their language was more completely developed. The degree of hearing loss was another factor that wasn't considered. People who have some residual hearing generally fare better in acquiring language.

Most eighteenth-century deaf people were not lucky enough to be taught by someone like Épée. Although deaf people and their families, friends, and acquaintances used sign languages, each region more or less developed its own version. There was little traveling between locations and no way that sign language could really be standardized.

By 1779, however—thanks in part to the efforts of Abbé de l'Épée—there was an active deaf community in Paris. Deaf people visited each other often and shared a common sign language. With one notable and surprising exception—Martha's Vineyard, which we'll discuss later—nowhere else in the world did there exist a real deaf community.

The standardization of the Parisians' sign language

happened naturally—just the way spoken language grows and changes. In talking about one another deaf people would describe a physical characteristic of someone—say a man named Pierre. If the man had a full, handsome beard, the person talking about him might rub his chin downward as if stroking a beard. Gradually that sign would be used by everyone talking about Pierre, and so Pierre's name sign would develop. Name signs are created in much the same manner today.

In 1786 Abbé Roch-Ambroise Sicard, one of the teachers trained by Abbé de l'Épée, opened a school for deaf students in southwestern France, in Bordeaux. Sicard taught a deaf man, Jean Massieu, one of seven deaf children in a family. Although Massieu did not begin his education until he was fourteen, his family had used sign language his entire life. Once Sicard began teaching Massieu, the boy worked at learning fifty French words a day, while Sicard made it a practice to learn the same number of signs from him. Soon Sicard would publish a dictionary of signs.

Both Épée and Sicard realized how grueling a task teaching speech would have been. Once, Sicard was asked why he did not work on speech with Massieu, his most brilliant pupil. He replied: "He might well come to speak if I had the time to teach him, but it requires so much painful labor and the deaf set so little value on it and use it so rarely, that I believe it is more useful to perfect their intelligence employing methodical signs instead." This view is one many deaf people hold today.

Abbé de l'Épée died in 1789, just as the French Revolution was beginning and religious people were being viewed with scorn in France. Yet Épée died with his reputation intact. His students said of him that he often would not take wood for his own fire because he wanted to make sure there was enough to keep them warm. By the time he died, he had used up all his own money. There were at least a dozen schools founded around France because of him. The National Institute was an important gathering place for deaf people. Upon Épée's death Sicard continued his mentor's work.

Massieu also became a brilliant teacher at the National Institute, and deaf people he taught went on to found many schools for deaf people around the world, including the first school in the United States. Massieu was a champion for the rights of deaf people. Ironically, after Sicard died, Massieu was the favorite to become the head of the institute. But oralists, led by a physician named Dr. Jean-Marc Itard, were coming in to impose their theories. Massieu was forced to resign.

Still, Épée's legacy was an important one, and today deaf people honor him for his willingness to try to immerse himself in learning their language and culture.

Despite these great strides made in the eighteenth century, the attitude of most people in Europe during the nineteenth century was that deaf people could not be educated. The French philosopher Condillac claimed that deaf people had no memory or abstract thoughts and thus could not reason. He changed his mind somewhat after watching students at Abbé de l'Épée's school. Still, after his death, his students went back to Condillac's original theory that without spoken language, people could not have abstract ideas. The public also held a low opinion of deaf people in part because educators, wanting to make themselves appear to be miracle workers, often undervalued deaf people's innate abilities. Deaf people's minds were called "blank." The difficult struggle for education of deaf people would continue across the Atlantic Ocean, in the United States of America, where incredible strides would be made—with the help of a Frenchman.

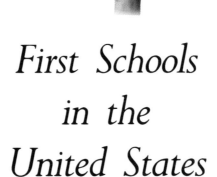

First Schools
in the
United States

On this side of the Atlantic there is little mention of deaf people in the records of the colonization of the United States. Life was too rough and tumble. Education for deaf people was not a priority among those fighting for their independence, and although there must have been plenty of deaf people in the American colonies, we know of very few.

There was Joseph Brewster, Jr., born in 1766, who became a rather celebrated portrait painter in New England. After his death his reputation dwindled—until the 1970's, when his primitive paintings fetched record prices at art auctions.

During the Revolutionary War a Boston man named Francis Green had supported the British side and was banished to England. Green sent his son, Charles, to the Braidwood School in Scotland in 1780, making Charles one of the first deaf Americans to receive a formal education. It was fashionable at the time for wealthy Americans to send their children to European schools, and certainly it was logical for deaf children of well-to-do families to go overseas since no schools for them existed in the young nation. President James Monroe's deaf nephew attended school in Paris.

Major Thomas Bolling of Chesterfield County, Virginia, had four children, three of whom were deaf—John, Thomas, and Mary. These three studied alongside Charles Green at the Braidwood School in Scotland. Major Bolling's son William, who was hearing, had two deaf children, William Albert and Mary. He had been pleased with the education his brothers and sister had received, and he would sponsor John Braidwood's unsuccessful efforts to open a school for deaf students in America in the early 1800's.

At the beginning of the nineteenth century Francis Green wrote to a New York government official praising his own son's progress, and actively urging that a school for deaf students be founded in the United States. He had previously written a 240-page book in support of Braidwood. After Charles was graduated from the Braidwood school, he joined his father, who had moved to Halifax, Nova Scotia. Something happened, however, to shake the family's belief in the Braidwood method. We don't know what it was. Charles lost his facility with speech, and the father and son came to prefer sign language for their communication. Soon the father denounced his book about Braidwood as a mistake—but even after Charles died in a hunting accident, Francis continued advocating public schools for deaf students. He wrote to ministers in New England urging them to conduct a census to find out just how many deaf people were in this country.

In 1810 a New York City minister, Reverend John Stanford, discovered several deaf children in an almshouse. He tried to teach the children, and urged the city to start a school for them. In 1818 the New York Institution for the Deaf and Dumb was founded with $10,000 and the promise of a lottery tax. There were sixty children enrolled.

But credit for the first continuously operating school for deaf students in the United States lies elsewhere. A Connecticut doctor, Mason Fitch Cogswell, who had a deaf daughter, Alice, had bought one of Abbé Sicard's books and given it to his neighbor, a divinity student named Thomas Hopkins Gallaudet. The book featured the manual alphabet that had been developed in Spain along with explanations for making signs. Gallaudet had taken an interest in Alice, who had become deaf around age two from spotted fever. He would take the hat from his head and write "h-a-t" on the ground. History doesn't record whether or not this was a breakthrough.

To support his belief that there were enough deaf children in the United States to warrant a school for deaf students, Dr. Cogswell undertook the census of deaf people in New England that Francis Green had proposed. The census found eighty deaf children in Connecticut alone, and the people helping Dr. Cogswell determined that there must have been four

Thomas Hopkins Gallaudet. Permission of the American School for the Deaf

hundred deaf children in New England and as many as two thousand in the entire United States.

Reverend Gallaudet's casual interest in Alice and deafness increased when, in 1815, Dr. Cogswell encouraged a group of wealthy Hartford citizens to send Gallaudet to Europe to figure out the best method for teaching deaf children. When Gallaudet arrived in Britain, he went immediately to the schools run by the Braidwood family in Birmingham, England, and Edinburgh, Scotland. He preferred the oral method of teaching, but he was disappointed to discover how hostile the Braidwoods and everyone who worked for them were. The Braidwood family forced employees to pay a thousand-pound bond of silence, promising never to reveal teaching methods.

They told him he could become a teacher in their school, but Hartford was awaiting him, and he did not want to sign a long-term teaching contract in Britain. The Braidwoods suggested that one of their own family members head the new school, or that John Braidwood, who was already in Virginia, could take over. Neither of these proposals appealed to Gallaudet, but when he received a letter from Alice, he realized he must get on with finding a way to return to the United States and start the school.

Not quite sure what to do, Gallaudet one day happened to receive a flyer announcing a lecture and demonstration in London by Abbé Sicard, assisted by Massieu and Laurent Clerc, a deaf student of the National Institute in France. Gallaudet was impressed by what he saw and talked with Sicard afterward, yet once more he went to the Braidwoods to ask them to relent. They would not, so Gallaudet went to Paris to study at the National Institute. The future of American education for deaf people was radically altered. Gallaudet persuaded Clerc to accompany him to America.

Many people tried to change Clerc's mind. Abbé Sicard angrily forbade him to leave, saying that Clerc should remain in a Catholic country and not go to a heathen Protestant one. Clerc's mother begged him to stay. But Clerc looked forward to the challenge.

He would be earning three times what he currently made. Although his contract would be for only three years, Clerc was determined.

On the slow, fifty-two-day Atlantic crossing, Gallaudet taught Clerc English and Clerc taught Gallaudet French signing. With his New England minister's sensibility, Gallaudet insisted on modifying the graphic French signs. What came off the boat in New England, though, was not watered-down French, but instead, through the collaboration of the two men, a true

*L*aurent Clerc. *Portrait painted by Charles Willson Peale.* Permission of the American School for the Deaf

American Sign Language (ASL). (Still, traces of French signing are evident in ASL. The sign *to see* is made with a *V*—two fingers radiating from the eye—for the French word meaning *to see*, which is *voir*.)

The two men established the American School for the Deaf, originally named the Connecticut Asylum for the Education and Instruction of Deaf and Dumb Persons, in downtown Hartford in 1817. Along with Alice, then twelve, there were six other students; the eldest, artist Joseph Brewster, Jr., was fifty-one.

Laurent Clerc was an elegant man whose sign name

An early view of the American School for the Deaf's original building. Gallaudet University Archives
∎

is made using the first two fingers brushing against a cheek. As a baby, Clerc had fallen into the fire in his family's home, and he had a large scar on his cheek. In paintings he always posed hiding this scar.

Clerc was so quickly competent in written English that he was soon writing fund-raising speeches. He became friendly with congressmen. After a demonstration by Clerc of his teaching abilities, Congress granted the Hartford school a 23,000-acre township in Alabama, which was then sold to raise money for the school's regular operating expenses. By the end of that first academic year, the number of students had grown to thirty-one, and over one hundred were enrolled by 1818.

Both Gallaudet, who was named principal of the Hartford school, and Clerc assisted in the founding and operating of other schools for deaf students around the country. During the nineteenth century many teachers of deaf students—deaf and hearing—were trained at the American School. At one point during the last century over forty percent of educators of deaf students were deaf, and the American School became very important because it provided a place for deaf people to come together and for their culture to develop. Essentially the school ignored lipreading and speaking techniques.

Clerc, it turned out, did not return to France at the end of his first three years in America. Instead, in 1819 he married Eliza Boardman, who had been one of the first students at the school, and together they started a family. Gallaudet, who had married Sophia Fowler—

Eliza Boardman Clerc, making the sign language letter e, *with her daughter. Also painted by Peale.* Permission of the American School for the Deaf
.

the fifteenth student enrolled at Hartford—retired from the American School in 1830. He devoted the rest of his life to writing and speaking about a number of causes, including the abolition of slavery.

And what of Alice Cogswell, the American School's first pupil? Alice was a model student, but after finishing her schooling she preferred to stay at home with her family. In 1830 her father, who was in large part responsible for the founding of the first school in America for deaf children, died. Alice was so upset at his death that she died a few days later of what many believe was profound grief.

While great progress was being made in deaf education in the United States, the situation in Europe was changing for the worse. Napoleon's defeat at Waterloo in 1815 meant that the rest of the European countries looked down upon all things French. The French method lost favor and was being replaced by the German or oral method.

Sadly, the British schools that had been begun by the Braidwoods were seriously run-down. As poor people flocked to the large cities, the schools were overwhelmed by the sheer numbers of students. Their education was abysmal.

Throughout Europe, education in residential schools for deaf students, then called "asylums," deteriorated. In Germany a group of teachers came up with a plan, which was, in essence, the first time "mainstreaming" was done. Deaf children who had learned spoken language would study alongside hearing children in school. However, the deaf children couldn't keep up, and the plan was soon abandoned.

In the mid-nineteenth century the case of Laura Bridgman did a great deal to heighten the general public's awareness of deafness as well as blindness. Laura Bridgman became deaf and blind at the age of two when she had scarlet fever. When she was seven, in 1837, she was brought to the Perkins School for the Blind near Boston to be taught by Dr. Samuel Gridley

Howe. Dr. Howe first worked with Laura by placing labels with raised letters on everyday items she used, such as a spoon and a key. The fact that someone who was both deaf and blind could learn was astonishing to the general public, and Laura, who spent almost her entire life at the school, teaching and doing needlework, was often featured in public demonstrations as well.

But society was still extremely biased against deaf people. As late as 1848 one writer claimed that they are "a grief and a shame" to their relatives, "a burden to society." Late in the nineteenth century one American educator said that if left alone, deaf people "would rise no higher than orangutans."

Laurent Clerc and Thomas Hopkins Gallaudet's work would have a profound influence on those attitudes. By the 1860's there were twenty-four schools for deaf students in the United States.

Schools have always been important for the spread of Deaf culture: *The American Annals for the Deaf*, the oldest educational periodical in the country, was started at the American School in 1847. In nineteenth-century America there were not many other places where deaf people could pass on stories about their historical achievements—but Martha's Vineyard was an exception.

When people migrated from Britain to New England, many families stayed close to each other in the New World. In 1657 a deaf man was born on Cape Cod in Massachusetts. His ancestors had probably come from the Kent region of England. The man

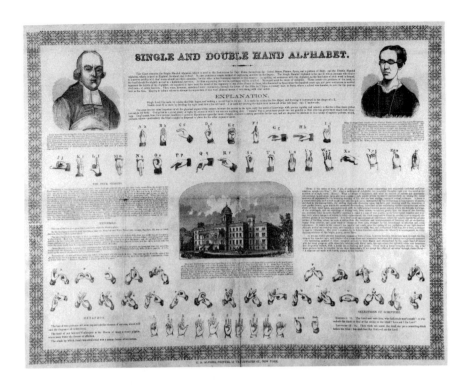

moved with his wife and family to Martha's Vineyard in 1692. Because the island was a small community, there were people who intermarried over the years. During the next twelve generations, from 1692 until 1950, a surprisingly large percentage of deaf people were born on Martha's Vineyard. One neighborhood had sixty deaf people at one time.

Deaf people on Martha's Vineyard had a sophisticated sign language that originally resembled English sign language. But this is what is so surprising: Because so many deaf people lived on the island, hearing people did not think of them as different. Nearly everyone on Martha's Vineyard spoke sign language fluently and naturally. Deaf people married, bore chil-

A sign language alphabet chart from around 1870. Laura Bridgman, shown in the upper right corner, was one of the first deaf and blind people to be educated in the United States. The abbé de l'Épée is in the upper left corner; in the center is the New York Institution for the Deaf and Dumb. Gallaudet University Archives

dren, held political offices, and had incomes that were similar to those of their hearing neighbors.

During the 1820's and 1830's, when deaf people from the island began attending the Hartford school, many things began to change. The sign language they used started to resemble American Sign Language (ASL) more, and because deaf people began to meet and marry people who were not from the island, fewer and fewer genetically deaf children were born. The last hereditary deaf Martha's Vineyard native died in the mid-twentieth century.

We should not think that all important nineteenth-century deaf people went to schools. Before any schools were established, one deaf man was making quite a name for himself in the wild West. Erastus Smith, nicknamed "Deaf" (pronounced "deef"), was born in New York in 1787, and grew up in Mississippi. He moved to Texas in 1821 and became a soldier. General Sam Houston was leading a revolt between settlers and Mexicans for control of Texas. In 1836 he chose Deaf Smith as his spy and scout. During the crucial battle of San Jacinto the eight hundred settlers faced sixteen hundred Mexicans under General Santa Anna. Smith told Houston that they ought to destroy an important bridge and force both sides to fight to the bitter end. Because of the settlers' triumph, Houston was named president of the Republic of Texas twice. Deaf Smith's picture was on the Republic of Texas' five-dollar bill, and a county was named after him.

Once somebody asked Deaf Smith if he was bothered by his deafness. He is said to have replied: "No, I sometimes think it is an advantage—I have learned to keep a sharp outlook and I am never disturbed by the whistling of a ball [bullet]—and I don't hear the bark 'til I feel the bite."

During the Civil War Northern schools for deaf students fared well, but several Southern schools were forced to close. Northerners destroyed the Mississippi school buildings. The Missouri school ran out of money. The Arkansas school was closed. Both Northern and Southern soldiers occupied several school buildings, including the Tennessee school in Knoxville. The Danville, Kentucky, school became a shelter for livestock.

In 1863 the head of the Hartford school and the head of a New York institution for deaf students made a trip to Europe to study education methods for deaf people. Although the Hartford school had hired a teacher for speech, the two educators decided that the strictly oral method was not satisfactory. Ironically, twenty years earlier, the Perkins School for the Blind's Dr. Samuel Gridley Howe and another famous educator, Horace Mann, had made a similar trip to Europe and concluded that the German, or oral, method was far and away the best. This debate would rage on into the next century.

C H A P T E R  F O U R

The Duel
Between Words
and Signs

Deep in the Civil War—April 8, 1864, to be exact—President Abraham Lincoln signed a charter authorizing Washington, D.C.'s Columbia Institution for the Instruction of the Deaf and Dumb and the Blind to begin a college course for deaf people. It was a historic moment. For over one hundred years the school that was first called the National Deaf-Mute College—and that would eventually be renamed Gallaudet University—would be the only college specifically for deaf people in the entire world.

It was a controversial college. One congressman claimed: "Higher education of the deaf is useless and of little value." In 1870 an editor of a journal on deafness published in Germany was aghast when he learned a college for deaf students had been founded. He ridiculed "the idea of the deaf and dumb being able to receive a collegiate, or even a high-school, education." In terms deaf people found appalling, he compared the idea of advanced education for deaf students to that "of teaching instrumental and vocal music to deaf-mutes," and he went on to say that he would "believe it possible when the blind become painters and the lame racers, when the palsied play the part of Hercules in the circus, when the deaf and dumb themselves become famous orators in churches and public halls!" He called the project "humbug!"

The prejudices of the ages are slow to change.

Because the federal government supported the National Deaf-Mute College and the tuition and room and board were very low, deaf people from all over the country could attend. In fact, because of the reasonable cost, in many cases the students were the first college-educated members of their entire families.

The school had come to be located in the northeastern part of Washington, D.C., as a result of the telegraph. Samuel F. B. Morse, a portrait painter, was married to a deaf woman, and to communicate he tapped messages into her hand. Morse combined that tapping with the idea of using an electromagnet, which had recently been invented, to create the telegraph. The very first telegraph message ever transmitted used the line that crossed the estate of Amos Kendall, whom Morse hired to be his business manager. Morse and Kendall became extremely wealthy as a result of the telegraph, and Kendall devoted much of his wealth to deaf people. He donated part of his estate to establish the Columbia Institution—and he also founded a church that held classes for deaf people.

From the beginning much of the instruction at the

school that would become Gallaudet was in sign language. This would help to fuel a bitter debate in the history of the education of deaf people.

Squaring Off—First, Bell

There were two men from strikingly similar backgrounds, both hearing, bearded, and contemporaries, whose extreme differences in opinion would continue to shake up the Deaf world for the next century. Both men had deaf mothers. Ironically, neither man was interested in a career working with deaf people early in his life. Circumstances radically changed the fates of Alexander Graham Bell and Edward Miner Gallaudet.

The inventor of the telephone, Alexander Graham Bell, was an unusually creative man. He developed many other inventions and was a well-regarded thinker during the nineteenth century. Bell was born in Edinburgh, Scotland, in 1847. His mother, Eliza, had become deaf during childhood. We believe today that she was not profoundly deaf but that she had a severe hearing impairment. She could use an ear trumpet, and she not only played the piano herself, but taught her children to play as well. She never used sign language and she was a very poor lip-reader. All her friends were hearing, not deaf. When people communicated with her, they would write, and she would answer with her voice, which was considered very good.

Alexander's father, Melville Bell, taught elocution and developed a system, *Visible Speech,* in which he

Alexander Graham Bell (at right), *inventor of the telephone and a believer in deaf people learning speech.* Gallaudet University Archives

created symbols to stand for each different sound.
Because of his experience with his wife, Melville did
not believe in stressing lipreading with deaf people;
however, Alexander Graham Bell came to feel that

lipreading was a crucial task for deaf people to master.

When he was in his early twenties, Alexander Bell—his friends called him "Alec"—was hired by a Boston school for deaf students to teach the Visible Speech method. He had enormous success with many of his students. But as soon as he encountered his first student who had been born deaf, he found the teaching more challenging.

Surprisingly, Bell was completely fluent in sign language, having taken a course in 1872. Still, he was an enthusiastic advocate of oralism, and so it was a highly unusual move for the American School in Hartford to invite Bell to come there to teach speech for two months. Later, the school asked Bell to give the commencement address, which he presented in sign.

In explaining his reasons for his support of oralism, Bell claimed that speaking kept families together while sign language created a barrier within the family when a child was deaf and the parents and brothers and sisters were hearing. Bell was an early supporter of day schools for deaf children rather than residential schools such as the American School and the many state schools for deaf students that had been established around the country.

Curiously, the telegraph played a major role in Alec Bell's life too, just as it had with Amos Kendall. Bell was working hard to find a way to send more than one message over a telegraph wire in the 1870's. In 1873 Bell was hired by Gardiner Greene Hubbard, a Boston patent lawyer, to tutor his sixteen-year-old daughter, Mabel, who was deaf. At the time Bell was twenty-six. Mabel had become deaf at the age of five from scarlet fever. As it turned out, Hubbard, who had helped found Clarke School for the Deaf, an oral school in Northampton, Massachusetts, was also interested in developing the multiple telegraph and supported Bell in his research.

Mabel was not at all impressed with Bell the first time she met him. He was disheveled looking and she did not think him a gentleman. Mabel was to change her mind not long after. She and Alec began courting.

Mabel's father wanted Bell to work quickly on the telegraph, and he made Bell an offer. If Bell would give up all his work with deaf people and devote his time to the telegraph, Hubbard would pay all of Alec's living expenses—and he could have Mabel's hand in marriage. Alec was stubborn. He said he would make a strict schedule for working on the telegraph, but he refused to give up teaching deaf children, promoting his father's Visible Speech method, and working with teachers of deaf students at Boston University. Finally, Mabel's mother encouraged her daughter to accept Bell's proposal, but Bell wouldn't marry Mabel until he was on solid financial ground. Mabel had to wait.

In 1876 Bell received his first United States patent for the telephone; he beat out another man by four hours. In 1877 he and Mabel married.

Some accounts say Mabel's speech was good. Others say she could really only be understood by her own family despite years of intensive tutoring. Bell vowed to Mabel that his interest in deafness would continue throughout his life; however, he refused to work on her speech. All accounts do agree that Mabel was an astonishingly good lip-reader. Her language skills were also remarkable. She was fluent in German and even acted as interpreter for her family when they traveled abroad. Mabel was extremely proud of her oral abilities, and she usually declined invitations to conventions where there would be numbers of deaf people. She avoided others who were deaf.

Bell, who was reportedly a likable, kind man, was a restless soul—often going off in several directions at once. All the while he was working with deaf children, he was continuing his research on inventions, which would eventually include the phonograph and the photophone. The photophone transmitted sound on a beam of light. Bell also held patents for hydroplanes and aerial vehicles. He invented the audiometer, which measured hearing loss. "Decibel," the word we use in measuring hearing, is named for Bell.

The year after his marriage, Bell started a day school for deaf children in a small town in Scotland. Five years later he founded a day school in Washington, D.C., with six children. The school had a class of hearing kindergartners on the first floor. Bell hoped the children would play together during recesses. This school closed after only two years.

At this point Alexander Graham Bell and his opponent in the debate on signs versus oralism were still on friendly terms.

The Opponent—Edward Miner Gallaudet

By bringing Laurent Clerc to this country, Thomas Hopkins Gallaudet was showing the world that deaf people could not only be educated, but they could also be professionals. Gallaudet lived a very happy life with the American School student, Sophia Fowler, whom he married. Sophia, who was deaf, was a lively, pretty woman who attracted many friends. She and Thomas had eight children. At home in Hartford the family used sign language.

Thomas Gallaudet first tried to talk his youngest son into a career teaching deaf children when Edward was only twelve. Edward had no interest in the field. He told his father that he wanted to go into business and make a great deal of money. But when Thomas died in 1851, Edward, then fourteen, was forced to earn a living to support himself and his mother.

He first went to work as a clerk in a bank, and later became a part-time teacher at the American School in Hartford in order to pay his way through college. In 1857 when Amos Kendall decided to set up a school for deaf students in Washington, D.C., the Columbia Institution, he asked Edward to come as superintendent. There was one requirement: Edward had to bring his mother, Sophia, to be the matron of the new academy. Edward was a surprising choice. He was only twenty years old.

At the beginning there were a mere fourteen boys enrolled. Sophia came along willingly and had a strong influence on the development of the students. Even though she herself had not entered school until she was nineteen years old, she was a role model for the young people. Because of his mother, Gallaudet was one of the first educators to consult adult deaf people

and to think about how they interacted with others and how they made their livings in order to figure out the best ways of teaching deaf children.

Congress provided the money to run the educational institution. Whenever the school needed a new building, Edward Gallaudet would have to go ask Congress for the money. One of the students wrote about what the school's president went through to make a good impression:

> Gallaudet . . . used to take pains to dress himself very neatly. He would put on his best clothes after having been shaved by his barber, [having] had a haircut and his shoes shined and finally [being] squirted with perfume. He used to have a team of horses drive him in a shiny elaborate carriage with great dignity and assisted by his coachman he would walk up to the front door.

After his talk to members of Congress Gallaudet would back out of the door with a big smile on his face, "bowing right and left."

The 1860's were busy years for Sophia and Edward Miner Gallaudet. Near the end of the decade Gallaudet decided to tour European schools for deaf students. On his way to Europe in 1867 he met Alexander Graham Bell and asked Bell to become a professor at the college. Bell had to say no because of his other duties. Obviously, their relationship was friendly at this point.

After touring fourteen countries Gallaudet observed that students from oral schools and those schools that used the "combined method" of teaching in sign and encouraging lipreading had similar abilities to speak. But he felt that students who were taught in sign were better educated overall. In the report from his trip Gallaudet wrote that schools should enroll deaf children at earlier ages than they had been doing. He also wrote that he believed students should begin instruction in speech and lipreading at a young age. In other words, he supported the "combined method."

Manualists—those who believed in teaching only sign language and ignoring all speech and lipreading— were outraged. How could Gallaudet betray them?

Gallaudet decided to set up a conference of principals in 1868 in Washington, D.C. He wanted the principals of manual schools to see the benefits of the combined method. But he didn't want those principals to be upset by the oralists, so he excluded oralists from the gathering on a technicality. In one way the conference succeeded: Many principals began speech and lipreading programs in their schools as a direct result.

In another way the conference was a political disaster. Oralists were deeply offended. They felt that Gallaudet had launched the first attack of a war— even though for the next decade and a half, more and more oral schools would be started, but no new sign language programs.

Still, Gallaudet agreed with the oralists that too much sign language was not a good thing. "The lan-

guage of signs in its present state of development,"
he wrote, "furnishes so easy and exact and beautiful
a means of communication between teacher and pupil,
that the temptation is strong to use it to an extent
which may operate unfavorably upon the pupil." In
addition Gallaudet was worried about deaf people
fitting into society at large. This attitude continued
to provoke manualists.

The year 1880 was an important one in the history
of deaf people. First, hundreds of deaf people met in
Cincinnati, Ohio, to set up the National Association
of the Deaf (NAD). The NAD has always been a strong
advocate of sign language and over the years has been
important in documenting sign language on film. It
has also supported the sign language interpreter
profession. The NAD is important to deaf people because they have been able to use the strength of the
organization to influence schools for deaf people. It
has also sponsored research and many, many books
and articles about deafness.

Just one month after the formation of the NAD,
Edward Miner Gallaudet and his brother were the
United States representatives to the 1880 Congress
of Teachers of the Deaf, in Milan. The major speech
at that conference was given by a follower of the
German oralists who ended his talk by shouting: "Long
live speech!" The Gallaudets were in the tiny minority.
Deaf teachers were not allowed to vote. The Milan
congress passed a resolution supporting oralism by
160 to 4.

Schools in Scandinavia, England, Spain, and Hol-

Dr. Edward Miner Gallaudet surveying the campus of the National Deaf-Mute College (to-day's Gallaudet University) around 1880. Gallaudet University Archives

•

land did not strictly follow the German or French methods until the Milan congress of 1880, when they switched to total oralism. This conference changed the course of the education of deaf children all over the world to the oral approach for almost a century.

In 1880, Alexander Graham Bell received the prestigious Volta Prize from France in recognition of his telephone inventions. He used his prize money to establish the Volta Laboratory, which was dedicated to work on future inventions. Later, in 1886, Bell sold several of his patents to fund the Volta Bureau, in order to support research and establish archives on deafness. The Volta Bureau promoted speech for deaf people and would become the headquarters for the Alexander Graham Bell Association for the Deaf, which to this day advocates oralism.

In this same year Edward Gallaudet asked that the National Deaf-Mute College confer an honorary doctorate on Alexander Graham Bell—the first honorary degree of his career. It was also in 1880 that Bell and Gallaudet, both members of an exclusive club, met at that club for dinner. Later Gallaudet would confide to his diary that the dinner had been "a sparring match," but the two men were still speaking to each other.

It was the next year that relations between them started to sour. At a conference Bell, who had promised Gallaudet he would support his ideas on the best way to educate deaf people, proved to be wishy-washy. The two men continued to appear before the same conferences and their correspondence was polite.

Bell's feelings about oralism became more and more definite over time. In 1886 Bell wrote Gallaudet a letter telling him he should not allow deaf teachers to work with deaf pupils. It was this issue that would ultimately lead to open warfare between the two famous educators.

Bell had founded the American Association to Promote the Teaching of Speech to the Deaf. In 1887 Helen Keller's father brought her to see Alexander Graham Bell. She was six years old and her father feared he would never find a good teacher for her. Bell began the process that would lead to the discovery of Anne Sullivan from the Perkins School. Anne would be brought to Alabama to teach Helen. In 1893 ground was broken for the new Volta Bureau building and Helen Keller, then thirteen years old, was an honored guest.

In 1889 Gallaudet College—the name had been made official—celebrated its twenty-fifth anniversary. That year the famed sculptor, Daniel Chester French, unveiled a bronze statue of Thomas Hopkins Gallaudet and his first pupil, Alice Cogswell. The $13,000 sculpture had been commissioned by deaf people who had donated the money from every state and territory of the United States. The sculpture shows Gallaudet teaching Alice the letter *a,* the first letter of the alphabet and the first letter of her name. There is a copy of the graceful sculpture at the American School for the Deaf in Hartford as well.

The next year Gallaudet petitioned Congress for $5,000 to start a teacher training department at the college. Gallaudet asked Bell to lecture at the school and Bell agreed—at least that's what Gallaudet *thought.* In 1891 both men were scheduled to testify before Congress. Gallaudet, in order to win Bell's approval, compromised himself by promising Bell that no deaf people would be allowed to become teachers of deaf students.

But when the two men addressed Congress, either Bell did not believe Gallaudet's promises, or he wanted to stab him in the back. He told Congress that he did not believe that United States government money should be supporting a school that was not strictly oral. Furthermore, he did not want a school in which deaf people might end up as teachers. The House and

Senate both turned down Gallaudet's request. "It is a pitiful spectacle, considering Bell," Gallaudet wrote in his diary, "to see a man of naturally generous impulses, given over to partisan spite."

In order to appear generous, Alexander Graham Bell asked a senator to give the college $3,000 to pay for oral instruction training. But Gallaudet grabbed those funds and started the teacher training college he had wanted from the beginning.

In essence, neither man won this battle. Gallaudet could not get the money for the department in a

A cartoon showing Dr. Edward Miner Gallaudet and Alexander Graham Bell squaring off for their fight over communication methods. The cartoon is from The Silent Echo *of October 1, 1892. Gallaudet University Archives*

straightforward way, so other people decided he was no longer as powerful as he once was. Bell decided that because Gallaudet used the money from Congress in a sneaky way, he was not to be trusted. Gallaudet felt that Bell had betrayed him. "Met Bell at the Capitol today and was glad of a chance to be cool to him," he wrote in his diary.

Alexander Graham Bell would make clear his feelings on signs when he wrote in the 1890's: "Then again people do not understand the mental condition of a person who cannot speak and who thinks in gestures. He is sometimes looked upon as a sort of monstrosity, to be stared at and avoided."

Over the next few months the men wrote back and forth, unable to come to any agreement on anything. Both were angry. Both felt their honor had been attacked. Gallaudet wrote in his diary that the hatchet was buried—but he knew where it was.

The anger worsened over another issue. There were two organizations of teachers who taught the deaf: the one that Bell had founded, the American Association to Promote the Teaching of Speech to the Deaf, and the Convention of American Instructors of the Deaf. Gallaudet wanted to merge the two groups. Bell, who was already distrustful of Gallaudet, didn't want the two to be combined.

In 1895 at a conference in Flint, Michigan, Bell announced he would go along with the merger by using a plan *his* group had created. In a later speech Gallaudet told the same audience that Bell had been a villain when Gallaudet had wanted to start his teacher training department at the college. Gallaudet said the bitter rivalry was all Bell's fault. He even had the sign language interpreter start at one end of the stage and slowly fingerspell the long name of Bell's group, the American Association to Promote the Teaching of Speech to the Deaf. There were giggles from the audience. Clearly Gallaudet was trying to humiliate Bell.

Bell was furious and stood up shouting after Gallaudet's speech. The audience was shocked. A school superintendent forced the two men to come forward and shake hands to show a public reconciliation. The men must have been clenching their teeth as they shook hands. Privately they continued their feud.

Bell wrote to his wife, Mabel, that he thought Gallaudet was "not quite sane. . . . I really do believe that he is suffering from mono-mania." Up until this time Mabel and Gallaudet had been friendly. Once Gallaudet attacked her husband, Mabel wrote him that their families could not continue to meet socially.

The
Battle
Continues

Edward Miner Gallaudet's basic philosophy was that deaf people were like everyone else. They simply couldn't hear. Underlying Alexander Graham Bell's philosophy was his profound belief that deafness was a terrible affliction that should be avoided at all costs. Bell wrote long papers saying that deaf people should not marry other deaf people because they would create more deaf people! One of the reasons he wanted day schools for deaf children was so that they would socialize with, and eventually marry, hearing people. Bell went so far as to say that in cases where deafness was hereditary, deaf people should not be allowed to have children.

Bell's efforts certainly had some positive effects. He advocated that the name given to deaf people be "deaf" instead of "deaf-mute." He argued that deaf people do not automatically have problems with their vocal chords, so they cannot be called "mute." Rather, they cannot hear their speech to monitor pronunciation. Bell also insisted that the nationwide 1890 census include questions that would help to determine the numbers of deaf people more accurately. And he felt that when a person became deaf late in childhood—say at the age of twelve—the speech this person had already developed should be preserved.

But largely because of Bell, for over the next hundred years the manualists (those who wanted to use sign) would continue to be pitted against the oralists. The number of teachers of deaf students who were themselves deaf dropped to about 15 percent by the turn of the century, when the oralist movement spearheaded by Bell was in full flower; even hearing teachers who knew signing were considered dangerous by many administrators. Those deaf people who were teachers were not allowed near small deaf children. In general they were only permitted to teach teenagers who were less academically gifted. That of course meant that deaf children rarely saw deaf people in important or professional jobs.

Some writers have speculated that if Bell and Gallaudet had found a way to work out their differences more calmly, then the teachers at the institutions they founded would not be so angry with each other to this day. Oralists who have followed Bell's teachings still accuse the manualists who follow Gallaudet's of sabotaging their work, and vice versa. Each group says that the other does not think about the deaf person as a whole.

In 1889, one hundred years after the death of Abbé

de l'Épée, deaf people themselves held an international congress. They were opposed to the oral doctrine passed by the Milan congress. They felt that hearing people were dominating *their* world. At this congress, held in Paris, a speaker said: "Suppress the language of signs and the deaf man is excluded from all society . . . he will be more isolated than ever." At the end of the gathering, in which deaf people declared that signs were their native language, they proclaimed: "Long live the emancipation of the deaf!"

In 1900 the International Congress of Teachers of the Deaf held its fourth meeting. Shockingly, the proceedings were segregated! Deaf people were not allowed in with hearing people. This was partly because the hearing people were afraid that the deaf people would vote down their resolutions on oralism that had been established in 1880 at Milan. Most of the hearing people at the congress simply did not want to learn about deaf people's ideas on any subject. The president of this congress, a Frenchman, had once written that deaf people were guilty of "idleness, drunkenness, and debauchery, easily duped and readily corrupted." This was a man who was supposed to be an educator!

Gallaudet and Bell were both present at the gathering and they immediately began exchanging angry charges with each other. Bell, who often had to lift the handlebars of his mustache so that people could lip-read him, announced the superiority of oralism. Gallaudet insisted the combined method was what was really being used.

When Gallaudet gave a speech, he infuriated oral-

ists by claiming they were immoral in their beliefs—
that they didn't really care about deaf people themselves, only their own theories. The language of the
most successful students, he declared, might be understood by their teachers and families, but not really by
the world at large. In other words, the oralist teachers
were not accomplishing their goals. The president of
the congress angrily imposed a time limit and stopped
Gallaudet before he'd finished.

A vote was taken on a resolution that read: "The
congress, considering the incontestable superiority of
speech over signs for restoring the deaf-mute to society and for giving him a more perfect knowledge of
language, declares that it maintains the conclusions of
the Milan congress." Oralists won the vote in over-

A nineteenth-century art class at the Illinois School for the Deaf, a school that taught children using the combined method. Gallaudet University Archives

whelming numbers, roundly beating those who favored the combined method.

By the last day of the congress emotions were running high. Gallaudet asked that the resolution be changed to say that only the *hearing* supported this resolution. He was turned down. Then the congress wanted to discuss how to protect deaf people after they finished school. Some advocated asylums for deaf women and government shelters and workshops for deaf men. These restrictions greatly upset deaf people, who did not want to lead their lives hidden away again. Besides, the oralists were supposed to be aiming toward integrating deaf people into society, not segregating them from it.

For nearly three quarters of a century, oralism would reign. Signing would be the guilty secret of the deaf world.

It is not surprising that the period from the end of the nineteenth century until the 1960's would be a relatively fallow one in deaf education. Deaf people, who had been making leaps and bounds in their careers and achievements, seemed to face terrible setbacks.

In the face of these challenges, one deaf woman's achievements stand out. Like Laura Bridgman, Helen Keller was both blind and deaf. Generally people concentrate on the fact that these women were blind, but for both these women, acquiring language was a crucial part of their education.

Laura Bridgman was the first woman who was both blind and deaf who was educated. Her breakthrough was considered very important since before then, people who were both blind and deaf were ignored. Helen Keller broke even more barriers. With the assistance of Anne Sullivan, who taught her the manual alphabet, became her sole teacher for many years, and remained her companion and interpreter virtually throughout her life, Helen Keller made incredible strides. She was graduated with honors from Radcliffe College in 1904. She wrote her acclaimed autobiography, *The Story of My Life,* when she was only twenty-two, and she went on to write several other books and to lecture extensively around the world. She worked tirelessly until her death in 1968 to improve the world for deaf and blind people. Keller once said, "Blindness cuts people off from things; deafness cuts people off from people."

The Twentieth Century Dawns

In addition to the oral and combined methods, a number of other ideas have been presented for teaching deaf children. One was the Rochester method, invented in 1878 in Rochester, New York. This basically meant fingerspelling for everything. The hand had to be held close to the mouth so that the person could lip-read and read the spelling at the same time. Spelling every letter of every word is an extremely long and complicated way to communicate; however, the system was used until fairly recently.

Another method was the Northampton Chart, which used printed symbols to show different sounds. Other systems used diagrams and different pictures to help deaf children understand language. Some of these were the Wing Symbols, the Barry Five Slate System, and the Fitzgerald Key. Variations of these and other systems are used occasionally in some schools even today.

Just before the turn of the century, scientists discovered that many deaf people have some frequency at which they can hear something—whether it is the very loud bang of a gun or a high-pitched squeal. Dr. Max A. Goldstein wanted to make use of this "residual" hearing, and so he developed the Acoustic method and founded the Central Institute for the Deaf in St. Louis, Missouri. In this method children are surrounded by different noisemaking instruments such as the harmonica, piano, and accordion. Goldstein encouraged children to feel vibrations and use their sense of touch to imagine what sound is like.

In the late nineteenth century people who were not completely deaf began using more and more elaborate devices to improve their hearing. One device that was popular was a ram's horn decorated with silver and ivory. This was known as an ear trumpet. Ladies might use a delicate fan cupped behind their ears. Some even used a large conch shell.

Other inventions included snail-shaped shells placed above the ears. A wire spring ran over the top of the person's head to hold the shells in place. People covered the shells and spring with their hair or a hat. Men with long beards sometimes wore a trumpet hidden under their chins. Tubes under their beards snaked up to their ears.

Some ladies had trumpets made to look like large hair combs. Rubber tubes ran from the combs to their ears. Men could even have the devices installed inside a fancy silk top hat.

The ear is a very complicated mechanism involving

nerves, fluid, tiny bones, and very fine hairs, or cilia. All these parts are required to conduct sound to the brain. In certain kinds of hearing loss, known as conductive loss, when the middle ear is affected, then some hearing can be restored by using the bones of the head as a conductor to the inner ear. Some scientists developed hearing aids that used the teeth to conduct sound. One that the Japanese produced in the 1880's was made of silk with a silver strip held against the teeth. Another creation was a two-foot-long metal rod. The person held one end against the other person's voice box. The other end of the rod had a section the person held in his back teeth. It must have been a very uncomfortable way to listen.

In 1900 the first electric hearing aid was invented by a Viennese man, Dr. Frederick Alt. Over the course of the twentieth century hearing aids would become smaller and more sophisticated.

In 1932 the Royal Residential Schools in Manchester, England, began using group hearing aids. The teacher wore a microphone and each child wore a hearing aid that picked up the microphone's signals. This method is still used in many classrooms around the United States.

Several oral schools used Alexander Graham Bell's father's Visible Speech method—until they realized that children were tracing the symbols in the air to communicate. Sneaking in signs has often been a problem in oral schools. In fact, in many oral schools teachers have been known to slip in a few signs when students didn't understand what was on their lips.

But because signs are forbidden so strictly, deaf children who do want to sign often feel guilty, as if they are doing something shameful.

The rise of the oral method was obvious in the early part of the twentieth century. In 1915, 65 percent of all schools were oral; 35 percent employed the combined method. By 1976 the trend was completely reversed: 35 percent of schools were oral and 65 percent were teaching by using the combined method.

A speech class at the Evangelical Lutheran Institution for the Deaf in Detroit, Michigan. The girl is holding her hand to her cheek as she feels the movement her teacher's cheek makes. Gallaudet University Archives

In addition to speech, the other skill that both oral and combined schools teach is lipreading. The best lipreader in the world actually gets only about 25 percent of what is spoken on the lips. Although some experts say the comprehension rate is as high as 40 percent,

that figure refers to understanding whole sentences rather than individual sounds.

Most sounds are made in the back of the mouth. Many words, such as "men" and "mud," look almost identical. Studies have shown that hearing people who take just one session of lipreading instruction do just as well as deaf people who have had years of training. Lipreading is a talent that some people possess and others don't, but having a good basis in language is helpful.

From early on residential schools offered programs to train deaf teenagers for work after they left school. Before the turn of the century most deaf men worked in farming. Women who worked outside the home were usually servants. As the twentieth century dawned, more and more deaf people were trained in other fields. Many young women were taught dressmaking and sewing. Men often learned the technical skills of linotype operation or printing trades. Linotype machines created the metal plates to print newspapers. The job was considered perfect for deaf people because the machines were so noisy. The work required a high degree of accuracy, and deaf people could make a good living at it. A number of deaf leaders in the twentieth century started as printers.

When World War I came, and so many young hearing men were drafted to serve in the armed forces, deaf men suddenly found themselves in demand for heavy work such as tire making. But as technology became more advanced and people began to rely more on telephones in the workplace, deaf people found

that they were at an extreme disadvantage. Attitudes proved devastating. As the general population began getting more of its information from the radio, deaf people had to wait longer for news and information. Deaf people were often hard-hit during the Depression, because jobs in general were scarce.

The first half of the twentieth century held many other heartaches for deaf people. Lawmakers tried to forbid them from driving cars, even though deaf people now are shown to have better driving records than the rest of the population. Insurance companies often charged deaf people higher rates for automobile and life policies. As new technologies squeezed them out of jobs, they worried about how they would make a living. In the face of these difficulties they continued

An 1892 typesetting class at the Horace Mann School in Massachusetts. Notice the type trays behind the students. Learning printing trades was very important for deaf people until computers took over typesetting work at newspapers and printing shops in the 1970's and 1980's. Gallaudet University Archives

•

Graduating Class 1925
Indiana State School for the Deaf

The 1925 graduating class of the Indiana School for the Deaf. Courtesy of Gale F. Walker

to attend the state and private schools for deaf people around the country and to seek the best employment they could find.

Once World War II began, the draft again caused deaf Americans to be in demand for jobs. Sadly, however, in Germany it was a different story. When the Nazis took over in 1933, they burned many books on teaching deaf and handicapped children. Deaf people would soon discover they were among the many groups persecuted by the Nazis. They were ordered not to have children, and many were sent to concentration camps. During World War II, 150,000 disabled people were put to death under Nazi rule; 1,600 of them were deaf.

By the 1940's there were 312 schools for deaf people in the United States, with a student population of 20,367. Sixty-five of these were public, residential schools with approximately 4,800 students enrolled

A cub scout pack in 1938 at the Indiana School for the Deaf, which had been founded by a deaf person and employed the combined method. Courtesy of Gale F. Walker

in them. Many of the residential schools used the combined method of teaching.

There were relatively few innovations in the education of deaf people in the forties and fifties, although the fifties saw the very beginning of film captioning. In captioning, subtitles are added to films, and a popular activity for deaf people soon became to gather at deaf clubs to watch movies with their friends.

Captioning would soon spread to other media. In 1971 the first television broadcast was captioned—a Julia Child program on cooking. By the late eighties almost all network programs were captioned. By purchasing a special device, deaf people had access to entertainment and television news just like everyone else.

A typical 1950's going-to-bed routine for girls in the primary school dormitory at the Missouri School for the Deaf. Gallaudet University Archives

As captioning became more sophisticated, the typewritten words moved across the screen even during live-action programs and the news. This same captioning device has been used more recently at lectures, where the speaker is shown on television and captions

are given for the person's text. Since 1993 all television sets thirteen inches or larger made or sold in the United States have been required to contain a computer chip that provides captioning at the flick of a switch.

As with the rest of the country the 1960's were a time of exciting changes. The Telephone Device for the Deaf (TDD) was invented in 1964. With the TDD—also called a Teletype (TTY) or Text Telephone—deaf people could finally use the telephone to talk with other people who had the device.

The TDD looks like a typewriter. A light attached to it flashes when the telephone rings. A caller places the telephone receiver into a cradle on the TDD, then types messages on a typewriter keyboard. The person on the other end of the line reads a printout or lighted display. Each person takes a turn typing, so that the phone call flows like a regular conversation. To indicate a sentence is finished, a person types, "GA," which stands for "go ahead." When the entire phone call is over, a person types, "SK," for "stop keying."

Today more and more businesses, hospitals, fire departments, and police stations have TDD's in order to communicate with deaf people. A Deaf teenager can call up friends to type out questions on homework or make a date. A major advance in telephone communication is the establishment of dual-party relay systems whereby an operator with a TDD acts as a go-between. A hearing person calls the operator, who relays his or her message to the Deaf person, and vice versa.

To make their conversations more personal, Deaf people have added their own touches to TDD conversations. If a person types something amusing, he or she will add "smile" or "grin" so that the other person will get the humor. The other person might type back "ha" or "smile" to show amusement. Parents might type "xoxox" to their children to show they are sending them kisses and hugs. If someone is displeased about something, he or she might type "frown." The word "you" has been shortened to "u" to make typing faster.

Because deaf people have to read and type so much, many deaf teenagers can type very well, better than the average hearing teen. Also, studies have shown that deaf people are better spellers than hearing people.

In the mid-sixties the Registry of Interpreters for the Deaf was established. Interpreters had to undergo training and certification. As schools, government offices, and hospitals realized the need for good communication, more and more sign language interpreters were available to deaf people.

In 1968 the National Technical Institute for the Deaf (NTID) opened at Rochester Institute of Technology in Rochester, New York. The college provided excellent technical training in fields such as photofinishing, accounting, and optical work, as well as training for certain factory and office jobs. Today NTID has almost as many students enrolled as Gallaudet University.

At about the same time, the National Theatre of the Deaf started touring the country with plays featuring deaf actors. The theater was showing hearing people what deaf entertainment was like. Sign language was a star.

One of the most important events of the sixties for signing deaf people was the research done on sign language. In 1965 Dr. William C. Stokoe, who had been chairman of Gallaudet's English Department, published *A Dictionary of American Sign Language*. He had worked with two deaf colleagues, Dorothy Casterline and Carl Croneberg. Because of this groundbreaking book, other researchers who had not studied

Joseph Sarpy and Camille L. Jeter in The National Theatre of the Deaf's production of Ophelia. A. Vincent Scarano. Courtesy of The National Theatre of the Deaf

sign language suddenly became fascinated by its possibilities. Studies showed that American Sign Language (ASL) was a language with its own system of rules about how words are put together and used.

Researchers soon realized that the sign language a person uses is on a continuum. On the one end there is American Sign Language. The word order is a bit like that of Italian, French, or Spanish, in which an adjective is placed after the noun. A person will sign "chair red" instead of "red chair" because it is important to let the other person know what the subject is. Also, in ASL the speaker must place the time of the action at the beginning of the sentence in order to set the scene and to conjugate the verbs that follow. Deaf people usually only use strict ASL when talking to each other.

At the other end of the continuum is Signed English, in which a person translates word for word what is being said in English. This can be a very laborious process because English consists of many words such as *of, the,* and *in,* which are incorporated within signs in ASL but which must be spelled out in Signed English. In the middle of the continuum is Pidgin Signed English (PSE), which is somewhere in between. Most people who learn sign later in life use PSE.

American Sign Language continues to be a treasure trove of fascinating discoveries. In 1991, for example, Dr. Laura Petito found that deaf babies who have deaf parents babble in sign just as hearing babies babble aloud.

At the same time that Stokoe was publishing his dictionary, educators began questioning the wisdom of the strict oral approach. Deaf people were unhappy about the results they were seeing in oral school graduates. They claimed the students had verbal language but that they didn't get a very good general education. They said deaf children educated at oral schools were too passive, that they let hearing people do everything for them.

Oral school supporters said that the education that signers got wasn't any better.

Professionals working with deaf people were seriously shaken up by a report delivered at the National Conference on the Education of the Deaf in 1967 in Colorado. The somber report began with this sentence: "The American people have no reasons to be satisfied with their limited success in educating deaf children and for preparing them for full participation in our society."

Educators thrashed about for a solution to improve the dismal showing. They came up with a new method: Total Communication (TC). There is no precise definition, but in essence, teachers and students were supposed to talk and sign at the same time. For two decades that system was seen by many as the answer to the manualist-oralist debate. Then deaf people themselves began to come into power.

Mainstreaming or Residential Schools? What Is Deaf Culture?

In the 1960's students at Gallaudet suddenly began talking about "Deaf Pride." Barbara Kannapell, a Deaf woman who has studied Deaf culture, started a "Deaf Pride" group to raise the consciousness level of deaf people. Some even say that the entire disabled community began to take pride in itself as a result.

In the 1980's deaf people began to capitalize the letter "d" to indicate people who were culturally Deaf. In other words, they were talking about Deaf people who wanted to be with other Deaf people, and who used sign language as the major way they communicated. What was clear was that they wanted the world to know that being Deaf was not second-best. The National Theatre for the Deaf had helped to show that sign language was a celebration, a beautiful, intricate language that created poetry in the air. Deaf people in the arts were flourishing. Not only were there deaf actors and actresses in the movies, on television, and on Broadway, but there were many more deaf artists, writers, and dancers.

There were also tremendous blows for Deaf people.

In 1975 Congress had passed the Education for All Handicapped Children Act. For almost all disabled children it was an enormous breakthrough. The law said that children had to be enrolled in school in the *least restrictive environment*. That meant that children who had disabilities would attend local schools along with everyone else. The system was called mainstreaming. Public schools had to make special teachers and tutors available and had to provide support services for children who were blind, deaf, hard-of-hearing, mobility impaired, or had learning disabilities.

Gallaudet's Chapel Hall around 1960. Gallaudet University Archives

The positive side was that children who were disabled could live at home with their families rather than in residential schools. Children had the opportunity to learn to accept one another.

For profoundly deaf people who had become deaf before the age of two, though, language was often a barrier. Adult deaf people worried about Deaf culture disappearing because deaf people would no longer be able to associate with each other while they were growing up. Deaf people said that instead of being included, as intended, they were more often excluded from outdoor games, school activities, and even instruction. Because teachers in classrooms turned their backs to write on the board, a deaf child who was lipreading might miss much of what was going on, especially when other children in the class were speaking. Or if a student had a sign language interpreter, the student might form a stronger link with the interpreter than with other students. Suddenly, 90 percent of all of America's thousands of deaf children were in a classroom in which there were not more than three other deaf children. In many, many cases around the country a deaf child who had been mainstreamed was the only deaf person in that entire school.

In 1982 a school district in New York State took a case all the way to the Supreme Court over the question of whether or not a school was required to provide a full-time sign language interpreter for a Deaf child, ten-year-old Amy Rowley. Amy, whose parents, Clifford and Nancy, are also Deaf, was an exceptionally bright child who had been mainstreamed. Her parents worked very hard to educate her; to go over her lessons at home each night. Although Amy received speech training and had two hearing aids, her parents wanted her to know everything that was going on in her classes. They had asked the school board to provide a sign language interpreter. The school board refused, arguing that Amy was doing fine in school. Her parents admitted she was doing well but said she could get even more out of her education with an interpreter. They hired a deaf lawyer, Michael Chatoff, to challenge the school board.

The case was a legal first. Never before had a deaf lawyer argued before the Supreme Court. In order for Chatoff to understand the proceedings, he had a special computer that displayed the questions the nine justices posed as a court reporter typed them. The Supreme Court said that school districts did have to provide special services for deaf and disabled children, but because Amy was doing so well in her classes, the district did not have to provide her with an interpreter. In a way it was a disappointing decision because it seemed to indicate that schools were willing to see that deaf people went only so far. The Rowley family soon moved to another school district in another state that did provide an interpreter, and Amy's education proceeded at a stunning pace.

Although by the late 1980's there were fewer strictly all-oral schools, enrollments at residential schools were dwindling because of mainstreaming. Deaf culture was in jeopardy.

*A*my Rowley to-
day, with her
brother John on a
vacation in Switz-
erland. She is a
student at Gallau-
det University and
he attends the
University of
Arizona.

In 1989 a group of disabilities activists recom-
mended that state funding to the American School
for the Deaf be stopped. They wanted all deaf children
to be mainstreamed. The response of the Deaf community was swift and angry. Deaf alumni and parents

of students at the school, which is the oldest "special" school in the western hemisphere, quickly sent a petition with 13,000 names to the governor of Connecticut. They turned out en masse at public hearings and demanded sign language interpreters be present at the public hearings. Dr. Harlan Lane, who has written many books on deafness, including a history of deaf people, called the school "the most sacred land for these people without a land." The quick action of the parents and alumni worked. Funding for the American School was left intact.

In the late eighties and early nineties, new technology created another controversy in the Deaf world. Medical scientists developed the cochlear implant. The device is surgically placed in the middle ear with a transmitter and receiver exposed behind the ear. It is not a miracle cure for deafness. With the cochlear implant some deaf people gain a perception of sound, but they must be trained to learn what the various sounds mean. The operation is very successful with older people who have lost their hearing.

Many Deaf people have objected to the surgical insertion of cochlear implants into young deaf children. They maintain that the long-term risks of implanting electrodes into children's heads are not known. They also say that it is unfair to force parents—many of whom do not know about the Deaf community—to choose for their children a partial life in the hearing world over a full life in the Deaf world, when they do not know their children's capacities. Some centers require an oralist approach for children with cochlear implants, and many Deaf people claim that Deaf children who aren't allowed to use sign language are, in effect, not getting any language at all. Language delay is very dangerous for Deaf children, they maintain. The National Association of the Deaf formed a study committee on the subject and issued a report opposing the practice.

Many pupils in high schools for deaf students discover that there are characteristics particular to Deaf culture. Deaf people need to have plenty of space around them so that they can see the hands, body, and face of the person to whom they're talking. If they go to a restaurant, they have to move the flowers from the center of the table to see and be seen when they converse. If they leave a room for any reason, they make sure to tell each other where they're going.

They don't have clues other people get from hearing someone's footsteps and other noises. For example, on dates, students like to go to bright places so that they can talk to each other easily. They do what other students do all over the country: go bowling or roller-skating, for example. But they don't usually go out to movies in theaters because they're not captioned. Summer leadership camps are important to deaf teenagers. So are deaf clubs, which are found in many cities in America. The very first deaf theater was not on stage; it was in deaf clubs and deaf people's homes. In other words, storytelling, with elaborate embellishments and poetic flourishes, is as crucial to the

Deaf world as it is to any group on earth. It is the way history and culture is transmitted. For deaf people storytelling is an important art form.

Deaf people often know a person's origins by his or her sign language "accent," and by the use of local signs. Although ASL has become increasingly standardized because of the mobility of Deaf people and the fact that so many have attended the same colleges, there are still telltale signs denoting a speaker's origins. One of the frustrations for hearing people learning sign is that Deaf people automatically "code switch"—they slow down the speed and complexity of their usual signing, often reverting to English word order—when signing to those who can hear.

Deaf people are a very heterogeneous group; they come from every background and every nationality. They can be rich or poor. As one medical anthropologist points out, except for the small percentage of deaf people born to Deaf parents, Deaf people—unlike people in other cultures—don't get their sense of identity in their own homes. When they talk to each other, they begin to realize that what is unusual about them is not their physical disability but how society treats them.

Deaf people often tell each other tales of discrimination. They are usually the last to be hired. Teenagers have discovered hearing people taking credit for their work. Residential school teenagers who go on to Gallaudet claim that students who were mainstreamed often ask them about Deaf history, who the leaders are, what the history is. Residential school graduates say they are more comfortable with their deafness.

There are definite disadvantages to residential schools. There is little privacy. Students know less about regular family life than do mainstreamed students. In the past the schools have been very paternalistic, taking over the students' lives and doing too much for them. Most schools have concentrated on changing that attitude and working on making deaf students self-sufficient.

Some Deaf artists and poets are militant. Ella Lentz's poetry urges hearing mothers to give over their children to Deaf culture. Dr. Betty G. Miller's early artworks include images of deaf children with marionette mouths, hands locked in old-fashioned stocks.

Today the state of the education of deaf people is being looked at from a cultural perspective for what is probably the very first time. One of the most radical theories is the bilingual-bicultural approach, in which children are taught mainly in ASL. For many years Deaf teachers were not allowed to teach in classrooms with very young Deaf children, but this approach encourages preschoolers and elementary school students to be in contact with Deaf adults.

Dr. Robert Johnson, head of Gallaudet's Department of Linguistics and Interpreting, says that it is nearly impossible for most people to sign and speak at the same time. Take the example of a hearing teacher speaking and signing at the same moment to a class of deaf children. Normally when that teacher makes an oral mistake, he or she will correct the error. The study shows, however, that the same teacher allows mistakes made in sign language to stand. That practice is very confusing to the students; the bilingual-bicultural approach avoids it altogether.

This new bilingual-bicultural approach is in place in a few schools in Sweden, Denmark, Uruguay, and Venezuela, as well as at the Indiana School for the Deaf, the Learning Center in Framingham, Massachusetts, and the California School for the Deaf.

After a hundred years of oralism, Dr. Johnson points out, average reading levels among deaf people are extremely low for a number of reasons. Total Communication (TC)—speaking and signing at the same time—caused a slight but insignificant rise in the figures. The average deaf seventeen-year-old reads at the fourth-grade level. Only 7 percent of seventeen-year-olds easily comprehend books written for their grade level. These figures include late-deafened people who are more likely to have a solid base in English.

Dr. Johnson proposes day care centers for very young Deaf children with Deaf care providers. And he and others in the field want to do away with the special language systems that have been invented to teach English to deaf kids, such as Signing Exact English (SEE), in which every prefix and suffix is given a separate motion, which many feel is enormously cumbersome in signing. Dr. Johnson points out that forcing Deaf children to tackle every subject from mathematics to geography in spoken or signed English—a subject they're also struggling to understand—makes learning enormously frustrating. Actually learning subjects, not just how to speak, is crucial if Deaf children are going to get on a par with hearing children, he says.

M. J. Bienvenu, a co-director of the Bicultural Center in Riverdale, Maryland, advocates shaking up traditional education in which the most "hearing" of deaf children fare the best. She says classroom placement should be based on ASL skill rather than auditory decibel loss. A Deaf woman herself, she puts an interesting twist on priorities: "Hearing parents of deaf children need Deaf role models."

Taking
Their Rightful Place:
The Gallaudet
Revolution

Great strides had been made in the education of deaf people before 1988. But it took the Gallaudet Revolution to make the whole world aware of deaf people's struggle for self-determination in their education.

When students at Gallaudet University closed down the school to protest the Board of Trustees' choice for a new president in March 1988, the trustees seemed shocked. They had no right to be.

For months Gallaudet students had been asking, encouraging—even warning—the board that Deaf people wanted to govern themselves. The students wanted a Deaf president for Gallaudet.

There were three candidates for the position. One was Dr. Elisabeth Ann Zinser, who had almost no experience with deaf people. She could not sign. The other candidates were deaf: Dr. Harvey Corson and Dr. I. King Jordan. There has probably never been any other college or university in history in which the students cared so deeply about who their leader would be.

On March 1, Gallaudet students and alumni held a rally in the football field. Over fifteen hundred people attended. Women's universities had women as presidents. Black universities had black presidents. Why couldn't the world's only liberal arts college for deaf students have a deaf president?

A national newspaper column had encouraged the board to choose a deaf president. Senators and representatives had written to the board to express their support. "The time is now!" people at the rally said. One alumnus passed out yellow pins that read: "Deaf President Now." The large group toured the campus, stopping at different buildings to let speakers address the crowd about the importance of self-determination. One student held up a hand-lettered sign that read: "Are you a racist? Earist?" The rally was exciting. People left thrilled with the prospects for the future.

The next day nine hundred students signed a petition, which they presented to the Board of Trustees, asking that a deaf person be named. Student body president Greg Hlibok wrote a letter to Elisabeth Ann Zinser asking her to remove her name as a candidate for the presidency. Students began camping out in front of an administration building, holding up posters.

The night before the board was to make its decision, students staged a candlelight vigil outside the board's meeting room. Some board members came to the window and gave a "thumbs-up" sign.

Sunday, March 6, the Board of Trustees infuriated

the entire student body by naming Dr. Zinser, the only hearing person of the three finalists, to be president of Gallaudet. They made a hasty announcement in a news release instead of holding a formal press conference. Students were outraged. Suddenly students, faculty, and alumni began a spontaneous march through Washington, D.C.

The police could not really communicate with the students, so they decided to escort the protesters as they marched to the Mayflower Hotel, where the Board of Trustees was meeting. The protesters sent messages into the meeting, but they were ignored for a very long time. Finally, the chair of the Board of Trustees, Jane Bassett Spilman, agreed to meet with three representatives. The meeting wasn't very productive, and the students—who felt betrayed by their own Board of Trustees—marched on to the White House and the Capitol Building.

Newspaper accounts of the meeting reported that Spilman told the representatives, "The deaf are not ready to function in the hearing world." She later declared that she had been misquoted, yet the newspaper accounts rubbed salt into the students' wounds.

Four students became the leaders of the budding movement: Greg Hlibok, Bridgetta Bourne, Tim Rarus, and Jerry Covell. All had lost their hearing very young. All had deaf parents. Their organizational abilities were incredible. In the past there had been many internal battles between groups of deaf people— sparked possibly by the history of conflicts that had begun back in the nineteenth century. But somehow these four students were able to get thousands of deaf people to work together.

On Monday students blocked all entrances to Gallaudet. Members of the Board of Trustees who could get through attended a meeting with administrators. Spilman had agreed to talk to a student delegation. She communicated with the young people through an interpreter, since she could not sign. At that meeting the students presented her with four clear demands.

First: Zinser must resign and a deaf person be appointed as president. Second: Spilman must resign. Third: The Board of Trustees must be 51 percent deaf. Fourth: There would be no action taken against the student protesters.

The board refused to accept these demands. Board members went to the field house to announce their decision to the students. Many students, furious, rushed out on a second march to the Capitol Building and the White House. Spilman stayed in the field house, and the remaining students began asking questions. During this impromptu meeting the fire alarm went off. The room was in chaos. Spilman couldn't bear the noise. Students smiled, saying the noise didn't bother them at all. "If you signed, we could hear you," they told her through an interpreter.

Every night that week there was a rally held in the gymnasium. TDD's were working furiously all over campus. Indeed, alumni and interested deaf people from all over the country were taking notice. They began to call in their support.

Newspaper reporters and television crews started streaming into Washington to find out about the protest.

"Deaf Power!" became an important sign on campus. By holding one hand over one ear and raising a clenched fist into the air, students were declaring their solidarity. Their protest wasn't just against the Board of Trustees. They were protesting the attitude barriers they'd faced all their lives. Students stuffed a sweatsuit, labeled it with Dr. Zinser's name, and burned it publicly.

On Tuesday the furor continued. Students held a rally filling the football field to capacity, chanting, "Deaf President Now!" On the Gallaudet campus are two schools for deaf children and teenagers, Kendall Demonstration Elementary School and the Model Secondary School for the Deaf (MSSD). Parents wanted to take their younger deaf children home. The children refused. The excitement was too great. They could feel that history was being made.

Still, some faculty and administrators didn't know which way to turn. Many of them were afraid of losing their jobs and supported the Board of Trustees. Many others felt the students had a very valid point.

Meanwhile, Elisabeth Ann Zinser decided it was time for her to leave her position as vice-chancellor at the University of North Carolina and come to Washington to confront the demonstrators and take over. She arrived Tuesday night.

Her arrival on Wednesday morning only added fuel to the fire. "I am in charge!" she announced, but students wouldn't let her onto the campus.

The faculty overwhelmingly voted to support the students.

Student leaders began meeting with congressmen and the press. Greg Hlibok and Dr. Zinser appeared on a national hour-long television program. He was calm, collected, and articulate. She said that "a deaf individual, one day, will be president of Gallaudet." Students responded with, "Why not now?"

The protest impressed people around the country for many reasons. It was nonviolent. No one was hurt. The students spoke only in ASL, while intrepreters used their voices to translate into English what the students were saying. Suddenly the nation saw that not only could deaf people band together on an issue; they could also be extremely well-spoken using their language.

Interpreters often volunteered their time. On their arms they wore masking tape arm bands so that students and campus security people would allow them through the gates. Contributions to support the student strike began flowing in.

On Thursday events continued to escalate. A large sign by the front gate read: "Honk if you support a deaf president." Everybody driving by seemed to honk. The deaf people could not hear the commotion, but the noise appeared to unhinge the hearing administrators. At rallies deaf students began applauding in a most unusual way: by holding their arms in the air and moving their hands.

Zinser did not have the support of the faculty. Realizing that what she was facing was not simply

student disapproval but a real civil rights battle, she resigned. It was Thursday evening.

On Friday morning she held a press conference announcing her decision. Then she displayed the shorthand "I love you" sign. She was gracious. She had been president for less than a week.

The struggle wasn't over. Students made up signs that read "3½." In other words they still had three and a half demands left.

Deaf people continued to pour into Washington. Busloads came from NTID in Rochester. People traveled from nearly every state in the union, from Europe, New Zealand, and South America. It was an aston-

Hands waving in the air became a sign for applause during the Gallaudet revolt in 1988. Gallaudet University Archives

ishing time for deaf people.

At noon on Friday there was a rally of three thousand people who marched from Gallaudet along Constitution Avenue to the Capitol. Proudly leading the march was a group of students carrying an enormous banner that read: "We Still Have a Dream."

Saturday was named "Board Buster Day." A picnic with free hamburgers and hot dogs was held in the beautiful spring weather. The DPN (for Deaf President Now) Council met twice a day to discuss strategies.

At last it was Sunday, March 13. The Board of Trustees had been meeting for nine solid hours. Finally that evening Philip Bravin, one of four deaf people on the seventeen-member board, went to the TDD to telephone student body president Greg Hlibok. The

Students' banner. Gallaudet University Archives

lights flashed on the TDD in the student protest head-quarters. Bravin, at the Embassy Row Hotel, insisted on speaking only to Greg. Students rushed out to find him. When Greg finally came to the phone, he typed his name. Bravin asked him a curious question: "What are the names of your brothers and sisters?" Hlibok answered. Bravin was asking for security reasons. Over the TDD anyone could be typing. He couldn't hear a voice to know it was actually Greg Hlibok on the other end of the line.

Finally, Bravin typed to Greg that Dr. I. King Jordan had been selected permanent president of Gallaudet. Jane Bassett Spilman had resigned from the board altogether. When Hlibok typed: "Who is Chair of Board Now Q [for question mark] GA [for "Go Ahead]," Bravin responded: "I am." Then he added there would be no reprisals against students. The students were overwhelmed with joy.

I. King Jordan made his acceptance speech the next morning, Monday, March 14. Jordan had become deaf at twenty-one from a motorcycle accident, yet he had thrown himself into learning about sign. As Dean of the School of Arts and Sciences, the unassuming man was extremely popular on campus. Lean and athletic, he is a Gallaudet graduate and professor of psychology.

"We know that deaf people can do anything hearing people can except hear," Jordan signed and spoke simultaneously in his acceptance speech. All around him were cheers and tears of joy from Gallaudet students. Greg Hlibok signed: "We have climbed to the top of the mountain, and we have climbed together."

Dr. I. King Jordan emerged victorious from the Gallaudet revolt.
Gallaudet University

‎.

Jordan continued to show what an unusual, thoughtful man he is. One of his first official acts as president was to talk to students at the elementary school on the Gallaudet campus. It was the first time a Gallaudet president had ever visited the school. "Maybe you'll grow up to be president of Gallaudet," he signed to a small deaf girl. The children had found a role model.

And now when deaf people get together anywhere in the country, they often applaud visually, their collective arms waving overhead like fields of wheat blowing in the fresh air.

Afterword

After the extraordinary events at Gallaudet the Deaf community was elated. The world as Deaf people knew it had been changed forever, and they were the ones who had changed it. Deaf people savored their freedom. They finally felt as if they were in control of their own destinies.

The ripple effect has been enormous. Canadians in particular took the goals of the Gallaudet revolt to heart. In May 1988 the "Deaf Ontario Now" Deaf Education Movement began across Canada. In October of that year protesters rallied in Ontario and at the Canadian Embassy in Washington, D.C. What they wanted was for the government to give more respect to Deaf people and to improve educational settings.

Many banded together to petition the minister of Education to release a long-overdue report on the education of Deaf children in Ontario. The minister delayed the report further and refused to meet with Deaf leaders. Much to his amazement, on December 15, 1989, Deaf students and community members marched into his office and staged a sit-in. They began releasing reports to the press saying they were disappointed with the level of Deaf education in Canada and requesting that American Sign Language and LSQ, or Langue des Signes Québecois (for French-speaking Canadians), be recognized as languages. Throughout 1990 hundreds of Deaf protesters demonstrated across Canada asking for educational reforms.

What happened next astonished the Deaf world. In September 1990 Gary Malkowski was elected to the Canadian Parliament, making him the first culturally Deaf elected official in the world.

His campaign was unusual: He was fighting for the rights of disabled people, Deaf people, and senior citizens, but he couldn't afford interpreters. He would often show up on people's doorsteps wearing a sandwich board. The front and back panels listed his ideas. As an MPP, or Member of the Provincial Parliament, Malkowski beat out three hearing people—including the candidate who had previously held the position. He now has four full-time staff assistants who are fluent in sign language.

In November 1990 the new minister of Education, Marion Boyd, announced that Ontario was committed to recognizing ASL and LSQ as languages of instruction. The minister quickly set up an advisory council on Deaf Education. Canadian Deaf people had won a rousing victory.

Gary Malkowski has become a highly recognized and effective advocate in Canada. One of his goals is to increase the number of sign language interpreters; interveners, or assistants, for deaf-blind people; and electronic notetakers who type what is being said in classrooms and at conferences in order to provide a transcript that Deaf people can read.

Onlookers were deeply moved the first time Malkowski stood to address Parliament. When he finished speaking, instead of clapping, members enthusiastically waved their arms in the air, just as people had at Gallaudet.

Many Canadians also said they wanted the "bilingual-bicultural" educational approach. Although certainly not all schools will adopt the approach, it has produced many positive effects for Deaf people in both Canada and the United States. Providing young Deaf children with Deaf adult role models is one; creating a friendlier atmosphere for Deaf teachers is another. Still, bilingual-bicultural education is a subject of hot debate in the Deaf world.

Since the Gallaudet revolt, legal changes benefiting Deaf people have been coming fast and furious. The passage of the Americans with Disabilities Act in 1990 has increased the number of situations in which sign language interpreters are legally required. The number of mainstream businesses with TTY or TDD telephone numbers has multiplied dramatically. And the law now requires dual-party relay services in every state—a major communication breakthrough.

The controversies that have surrounded the Deaf world for so many years will probably rage for a long time to come. But many Deaf leaders feel it's healthy to have these kinds of passionate debates. They provoke new thinking. They lead to excitement. They may lead to new success stories.

What are some of the other effects of the Gallaudet revolt? Deaf people are assuming positions of power in new fields. There are more white-collar Deaf workers than ever. Suddenly there is an increase in Deaf government officials in high positions, in Deaf stockbrokers and accountants and lawyers. Deaf activists are working toward setting up more rest homes for elderly Deaf people. They are creating programs so that hearing parents of Deaf babies can meet Deaf adults and see that there is a real future for their children. Deaf adults are establishing mentor relationships with Deaf youngsters in an effort to reach out to them, to bring the Deaf world—which has been badly splintered—together.

Deaf people are even more excited about banding together to celebrate their culture. There is even a cruise line that offers special trips for Deaf people so that they can visit Caribbean islands or glacial fjords with guides who speak sign language or with competent onboard sign language interpreters. The cruise line's motto is: "Thousands of waving hands." And more and more Deaf people have embraced the powerful message of Dr. I. King Jordan: "Deaf people can do anything—except hear."

Twentieth-Century Deaf People of Achievement

Because of the enormous social and technological changes in the twentieth century, a vast number of deaf people have made significant achievements in many fields. In particular, a number of deaf people came into prominence in the 1970's, when the Deaf world was bristling with activity. Several enrolled in law schools around the country. Others became dentists, government officials, actors and actresses, playwrights, writers, and activists. This is only a partial listing. Many of these people have made major contributions to several fields.

Performing Arts

A number of deaf people have appeared on stage, screen, and television in recent years. As a New York City high-school senior, **Bruce Hlibok** had a starring role in *Runaways,* a long-running Off-Broadway production of the seventies. Bruce comes from a socially active family; his brother, Greg, was one of the student leaders of the Gallaudet revolt.

Lou Ferrigno, who has a 65 percent hearing loss, had his own television series, *The Incredible Hulk*. Once

B*ruce Hlibok*

a shy child who was tormented by others, he took up weight lifting to play the 270-pound muscleman.

Linda Bove was the first Deaf actress to have a continuing role in a television series. She has appeared on "Sesame Street" since the seventies. A Gallaudet graduate, she had been with the National Theatre of the Deaf for a decade prior to joining the popular television program.

As Deaf performers around the country began searching for outlets, **New York Deaf Theatre,** established in 1979, not only provided professional quality plays; it has also held an annual Deaf playwrights' competition.

Bernard Bragg, a professor at Gallaudet, is well-regarded in the Deaf community for his acting skills. He studied pantomime with Marcel Marceau and has performed his one-man mime shows throughout the

New York Deaf Theatre: Elena Blue (left) and Alan Barwiolek (right) in A Christmas Carol

United States and Europe. Bragg, who holds an honorary doctorate from Gallaudet, has appeared on national television many times and even had his own series, *The Quiet Man*.

In the early eighties **Phyllis Frelich** created a sensation on Broadway in her role in the play *Children of a Lesser God*. She was the first deaf person to win a Tony Award. In 1986 **Marlee Matlin** was the first deaf actress to win an Academy Award when the play became a movie.

Phyllis Frelich

Marlee Matlin
Greg Gorman
.

Sports

Competitive figure skating is one of the most beautiful and grueling sports in the world. It requires grace, agility, stamina, balance, and a real feeling for music and rhythm. **David Michalowski** confounded the skating world with his flawless performances in international competitions. Profoundly deaf since birth, he memorized each work of music in order to perform. He is an extraordinary craftsman on the ice.

In 1976 **Kitty O'Neil**, a deaf Hollywood stuntwoman, set a land speed record for women in a rocket-powered race car, hitting 512.083 mph. She also established a record in 1970 for the fastest woman on water skis—104.85 mph.

David
Michalowski

Chroniclers of the Deaf Experience

Two deaf writers in particular have added to the growing volumes on Deaf culture: **Martin L. A. Sternberg** spent nearly two decades working on *American Sign Language: A Comprehensive Dictionary*. This important work, which includes foreign-language indexes, gave colleges and high schools a textbook for their courses in American Sign Language, and helped spur the movement to recognize ASL as a foreign language in a number of high schools and colleges around the country.

Dr. Martin L. A. Sternberg William Cunningham
.

Jack Gannon's book *Deaf Heritage* was the first true history of deaf people, and it gave deaf people a

*Dr. Jack R.
Gannon* Gallaudet
University
∎

real sense of cohesion as a group. His book detailing the events of the Gallaudet uprising in 1988 has also become an important resource in the Deaf world.

Ella Mae Lentz, who has participated in many studies of ASL linguistics, is a renowned poet in sign language.

*J*ohn T. C. Yeh

Business

John Yeh, along with two hearing brothers, started a computer business, Integrated Microcomputer Systems. Yeh is president and many of the employees are deaf.

Education and Public Service

In 1974 **Alice Hagemeyer,** a deaf librarian at a Washington, D.C., library, organized a Deaf Awareness Week. The program quickly spread to other libraries around the country.

Robert R. Davila rose to become a high-ranking government official in the Department of Education in the eighties and nineties.

Frank Bowe served as chairperson of the U.S. Congress Commission on Education of the Deaf from 1986 to 1988. The Commission studied education of deaf children and made recommendations that rapidly

*A*lice *Hagemeyer*

led to improvements in the quality of education for deaf children in America. An educator and the author of several books, Dr. Bowe is also an expert on rehabilitation.

Overseeing the education of other deaf people has been an important goal for many leaders in the United States. For a number of years there were no deaf school superintendents in the country. Today there is a movement to have more deaf people in positions of power in schools for deaf people. Superintendents of

*D*r. Robert R. *Davila*
.

schools who are deaf include **Gertrude Galloway** of the Marie H. Katzenbach School for the Deaf in New Jersey, one of the first deaf women superintendents, and **Harvey J. Corson,** who went on to become provost at Gallaudet University in 1988.

Gary Malkowski became the first culturally Deaf elected official in the world in September 1990, when

*G*ertrude
Galloway
.

*G*ary *Malkowski*
.

Philip Bravin Gallaudet University

.

he was elected to the Canadian parliament.

Gallaudet, of course, has trained and employed many of the world's brightest deaf people. **Philip Bravin** is the head of the Board of Trustees. Another important twentieth-century deaf figure is **Irving King Jordan, Jr.,** but it required a revolution that took the nation by storm for Philip Bravin, Dr. Corson, and Dr. Jordan to be able to take their well-earned posts at Gallaudet University.

Acknowledgments

Over the years I have had the privilege of speaking with many people whose opinions have informed this book. Martin L. A. Sternberg has always been supportive. I had intriguing talks with the distinguished author Harlan Lane; Robert Johnson, head of Gallaudet's Department of Linguistics and Interpreting; Deaf leader Barbara Kannapell (over the TDD); artist Betty Miller; historian John Vickery Van Cleve; medical anthropologist Nora Ellen Groce; and several people at the American School for the Deaf, including Winfield McChord, Jr., and Assistant Dean Fern Reisinger.

At the height of the Gallaudet Revolution fervor I had the benefit of talks with Roz Rosen, Bridgetta Bourne, Greg Hlibok, Tim Rarus, and Jack Gannon. I found Eddy Laird and Rachel Stone, superintendent and principal of the Indiana School for the Deaf, to have refreshing ideas for educating young Deaf people. In addition, I'd like to thank Alan Barwiolek and Alan Ander for their interest and support.

Certainly I am grateful to my parents, Gale and Doris Walker, for the many, many ways in which they have helped me.

I wish to thank Dr. Frank Bowe for his extremely careful review of this manuscript. Cynthia Kane, the editor of this book, has shown an unflagging enthusiasm for the subject. Her thoughtful editing brought the book alive.

I consulted numerous books and articles in the course of my research, and they are listed in the bibliography. The following were especially helpful: *When the Mind Hears* by Harlan Lane, a MacArthur Fellow; Oliver Sacks's *Seeing Voices;* Beryl Lieff Benderly's *Dancing Without Music;* Jack R. Gannon's *The Week the World Heard Gallaudet* and *Deaf Heritage;* and Richard Winefield's *Never the Twain Shall Meet* about Edward Miner Gallaudet and Alexander Graham Bell.

Bibliography

If you are interested in learning more about deaf people, their history, and their culture, try some of these books. Titles with an asterisk (*) may be of special interest to young readers and are annotated.

Bell, Alexander Graham. *Memoir Upon the Formation of a Deaf Variety of the Human Race*. Washington, D.C.: private printing, 1883.

Bender, Ruth. *The Conquest of Deafness: A History of the Long Struggle to Make Possible Normal Living to Those Handicapped by Lack of Normal Hearing*. Cleveland: Case Western Reserve University Press, 1970.

*Benderly, Beryl Lieff. *Dancing Without Music: Deafness in America*. Garden City, New York: Anchor Press/Doubleday, 1980.
A researcher explains scientific and cultural details about deaf people.

Gallaudet, Edward Miner. *History of the College for the Deaf: 1857–1907*. Washington, D.C.: Gallaudet College Press, 1983.

*Gannon, Jack R. *Deaf Heritage: A Narrative History of Deaf America*. Silver Spring, Maryland: National Association of the Deaf, 1981.

A thorough, groundbreaking look at the many accomplishments of deaf people.

*————. *The Week the World Heard Gallaudet.* Washington, D.C.: Gallaudet University Press, 1989.
A stirring tribute to the 1988 Gallaudet revolt in photographs with text.

*Groce, Nora Ellen. *Everyone Here Spoke Sign Language: Hereditary Deafness on Martha's Vineyard.* Cambridge, Massachusetts: Harvard University Press, 1985.
From about 1650 to 1950 Martha's Vineyard had a large deaf population. This book explains how they were "just like everybody else."

Higgins, Paul C. *Outsiders in a Hearing World: A Sociology of Deafness.* Beverly Hills: Sage Publications, 1980.

*Keller, Helen. *The Story of My Life.* New York: New American Library, 1988.
Helen Keller, who became blind and deaf as a toddler, was a pioneer in getting the world to understand that blind and deaf people can accomplish great things.

Klima, Edward, and Ursula Bellugi. *The Signs of Language.* Cambridge, Massachusetts: Harvard University Press, 1979.

Lane, Harlan. *The Mask of Benevolence: Disabling the Deaf Community.* New York: Knopf, 1992.

*————. *When the Mind Hears: A History of the Deaf.* New

York: Random House, 1976.
An intriguing history written mainly from the perspective of Laurent Clerc, one of the world's first deaf teachers.

————, editor. Translated by Franklin Philip. *The Deaf Experience: Classics in Language and Education.* Cambridge, Massachusetts: Harvard University Press, 1984.

Neisser, Arden. *The Other Side of Silence: Sign Language and the Deaf Community in America.* New York: Alfred A. Knopf, 1983.

Padden, Carol, and Tom Humphries. *Deaf in America: Voices from a Culture.* Cambridge, Massachusetts: Harvard University Press, 1988.

*Sacks, Oliver. *Seeing Voices: A Journey into the World of the Deaf.* Berkeley: University of California Press, 1989.
A neurologist explores the deaf world.

Schein, Jerome D., and Marcus T. Delk. *The Deaf Population of the United States.* Silver Spring, Maryland: National Association of the Deaf, 1974.

Stokoe, William C., editor. *Sign and Culture: A Reader for Students of American Sign Language.* Silver Spring, Maryland: Linstok Press, 1980.

*Walker, Lou Ann. *A Loss for Words.* New York: HarperCollins, 1986.
An autobiographical look at what it is like for a hearing child with deaf parents to bridge the hearing and deaf worlds.

Winefield, Richard. *Never the Twain Shall Meet: Bell, Gallaudet, and the Communications Debate*. Washington, D.C.: Gallaudet University Press, 1987.

*Wright, David. *Deafness*. New York: Stein & Day, 1969.
Wright, a deaf poet and Englishman who grew up an oralist, tells the story of his life.

Recommended Books for Younger Readers

Booth, Barbara D. *Mandy*. Illustrated by Jim LaMarche. New York: Lothrop, Lee & Shepard, 1991.
A lovely story, beautifully illustrated, about a determined deaf girl and her grandmother.

Riskind, Mary. *Apple Is My Sign*. Boston: Houghton Mifflin, 1981.
A 10-year-old deaf boy, Harry, from an all-deaf family, goes off to school in Philadelphia at the turn of the century. This book is about his experiences encountering the hearing world for the first time.

Scott, Virginia M. *Belonging*. Washington, D.C.: Gallaudet University Press, 1986.
A teenage girl who has a hearing loss tries very hard to fit in at school.

Walker, Lou Ann. *Amy: The Story of a Deaf Child*. Photographs by Michael Abramson. New York: E. P. Dutton, 1985.
Amy Rowley, an eleven-year-old deaf girl, tells in her own words what her life is like.

Books on Sign Language

If you'd enjoy learning about sign language, these are excellent resources.

Ancona, George, and Mary Beth. *Handtalk Zoo*. Photographs by George Ancona. New York: Four Winds Press, 1989. How to sign the names of various animals and how to tell time in sign.

Charlip, Remy, and Mary Beth. *Handtalk: An ABC of Finger Spelling and Sign Language*. Photographs by George Ancona. New York: Four Winds Press, 1974. A few signing basics cheerfully presented in color photographs.

————. *Handtalk Birthday*. Photographs by George Ancona. New York: Four Winds Press, 1987. A deaf woman celebrates her birthday in sign.

Costello, Elaine. *Signing: How to Speak with Your Hands*. New York: Bantam Books, 1983. A good basic primer on signing.

Rankin, Laura. *Handmade Alphabet*. Dial Books: New York, 1991. A poetically beautiful presentation of the manual alphabet.

Sternberg, Martin L. A. *American Sign Language Dictionary*. New York: HarperCollins, 1987. This pioneering dictionary is available in comprehensive and condensed versions. The drawings and directions are clear and easy to follow.

Index

Boldface page numbers refer to illustrations

About the Author

Lou Ann Walker grew up as one of three hearing daughters of Deaf parents, an experience she describes in her acclaimed book *A Loss for Words: The Story of Deafness in a Family*. She is a lecturer and consultant in the field of deafness. As a certified sign language interpreter she has appeared on national television signing for President Carter, and she has signed in courts, hospitals, and classrooms.

Ms. Walker is also the author of *Amy: The Story of a Deaf Child* and *Roy Lichtenstein: The Artist at Work*, both photographed by Michael Abramson. In addition she has written numerous articles for national publications, including *The New York Times Magazine, Esquire, Parade*, and *Life*. She was awarded a National Endowment for the Arts grant for creative writing.

She lives in Sag Harbor, New York, with her husband, writer Speed Vogel, and their daughter, Kate.